SUCCEED WITH YOUR TEAM

For a complete list of Management Books 2000 titles
visit our web-site on http://www.mb2000.com

SUCCEED WITH YOUR TEAM

BUILD YOUR STAFF INTO A HIGH PERFORMING TEAM IN 4 HOURS

Rupert Eales-White

2000

First published in 2010 by Management Books 2000 Ltd
Forge House, Limes Road
Kemble, Cirencester
Gloucestershire, GL7 6AD, UK
Tel: 0044 (0) 1285 771441
Fax: 0044 (0) 1285 771055
Email: info@mb2000.com
Web: www.mb2000.com

British Library Cataloguing in Publication Data is available

ISBN 9781852526405

Contents

Dedication to Gavin Cushny, né Eales-White 7

Foreword 9

Introduction 13

1 Tools and Techniques 29

2 Prepare to Succeed 45

3 Create the Right Environment 53

4 Promote Group Discovery 61

5 Harness the Power of Process 77

6 Recipe for Action 103

7 Break Free from "Received Wisdom" 105

8 Create Growth from Change 125

9 Manage Effective Feedback 149

Appendix 1. Project Omega for Organisations 155

Appendix 2. Project Omega for Education 163

Dedication

This book and the entire series are dedicated to the memory of my beloved brother Gavin Cushny. Gavin was murdered on 11th September 2001 by Osama Bin Laden. He was working on the 104th floor of the North Tower, which the first Boeing hit. Gavin was a man of enormous courage, indomitable will and hunger for life. Though trapped above the Boeing, he nearly broke free from the building. His body was found in a stairwell with another victim and twelve of those incredibly brave New York firemen. He did not die alone.

Foreword

Building high performance teams is of key importance to managers and there are many books on the subject – so why do we need another one?

Succeed with Your Team is different in that it is deliberately targeted at action-oriented line managers who want to understand not only *what* to do to build their teams, but *why* some approaches work and others don't. Managers who absorb the lessons of the book and put them into practice can achieve great things, without needing to call on external support.

This is not a classic textbook. Rupert's style is personal, conversational, often humorous and sometimes irreverent. He is not afraid to admit to his own mistakes and the book is the richer for the lessons he learns.

He also does not hesitate to identify some commonly held theories and assumptions about team building which generally do not work. Some of the well-known management gurus come in for criticism, not least those with a predominantly academic (or scientific) perspective.

In particular, Rupert highlights the consequences of 'typecasting' which can result from amateur use of Meredith Belbin's frequently used team role questionnaire. Over-emphasising differences between individuals can not only damage co-operation and creative synergy within the team but can stunt personal growth for the individuals within it. Yet, for many people, the main takeaway from a team-building exercise is their Belbin type.

This is not to say that the book is anti-academic. Rupert's interest in ideas and philosophies ensures that the methodology is properly underpinned by theory and academic research. Above all, it focuses on what has been thoroughly tested and shown to work in the real world, often in demanding circumstances.

I can attest to Rupert's skill and insight in helping often disparate groups of people to bond and work effectively together. My first encounter was in the early 1990's when I commissioned from a leading Management Centre a programme to develop the commercial and managerial skills of newly-promoted partners in a major international law firm.

The concept of management development for lawyers was then not generally accepted (and indeed the concept of *management* itself in a law firm context was regarded by many lawyers as curious, to say the least.)

The programme was a high-risk experiment, and several of the very individualistic lawyers on this one-week residential programme openly questioned why they needed to be there – it was by no means certain that all would stay the course.

For the programme to succeed, the highly respected faculty would have to demonstrate the relevance of what they were teaching (and quickly).

The programme was, thankfully, a success but only some of the faculty really rose to the challenge, and built trust and rapport. Of these, Rupert stood out for his empathy and ability to promote team-working.

Following this early win, Rupert went on to design and deliver programmes for further groups of partners and subsequently for many other groups from all over the worldwide firm. The basic principles and approach worked every time, across job levels and national cultures.

The key to this success, in my opinion, was the development of a set of techniques which use the full resources of the mind by drawing out and integrating the logical (left-brained) and the intuitive (right-brained).

When these techniques have been practised sufficiently to become habitual, they result in huge leaps forward in creativity and decision-making. They also refresh the parts other approaches cannot reach, building strength and confidence both for the team and the individual.

Creating and being part of a great team produces better results, makes work more rewarding and helps people to grow. Good managers want this for themselves and those who work with them. *Succeed with Your Team* provides all the guidance needed to turn aspiration into reality and I commend it to you.

Martin Pexton
Personnel Director of Allen & Overy (a premier global law firm) 1990-2002; Corporate Development Director of London Merchant Securities plc (a FTSE 250 real estate and private equity company) 2002-2007; Managing Director LMS Capital plc (a leading private equity company) 2007–2009.

Introduction

INTRODUCTION

"The received wisdom or conscious collective mindset, universally held, that the individual creates the team denies effective team-working taking place in the work-place. This book explodes that myth and proves, beyond a shadow of a doubt, that it is, in fact, the team that creates the individual. The discovery of this new paradigm enabled me to develop and successfully apply to over 1000 groups a recipe that enables any manager anywhere in the world to build a high-performing team in the work-place in 4 hours."

The objective of this book is to enable you to build any group, where you have a team-leadership role, into a winning or high-performing team in your place of work in 4 hours.

In this introduction, we cover:

❑ The results of building a winning team in the work-place.
❑ The benefits for you.
❑ My voyage of discovery.
❑ Why the recipe is unique.
❑ How the objective is achieved for you.

THE RESULTS

The results of building your group(s) into a winning team in the work-place are:

❑ The output and effectiveness of a high-performing team is always greater than the sum of its individual parts – what is termed, "synergy". You will get better results faster than before.

❑ As part of the process of creating your winning team, you will produce an action plan to progress your most important strategic issue. Your team-members will be highly motivated to ensure rapid and successful implementation of that plan.

❑ Your team-members will become a great support to each other and to you.

THE BENEFITS FOR YOU

The benefits for you are that:

❑ Your career prospects will be enhanced. Bosses tend to reward direct reports who produce outstanding performance for them, as they can, rightly, shine in reflected glory.

❑ Office politics will be minimised within your area of control.

❑ The work environment or local culture will be very positive – everyone will have high job satisfaction and energy levels.

❑ Your quality of working life will improve.

❑ You will be able to achieve, what has hitherto been extremely elusive for most, a real work-life balance.

MY VOYAGE OF DISCOVERY

I split this into two sections – my career in banking and my career as a development consultant.

CAREER IN BANKING

I was brought up to be and behaved in my early years at work as an individualistic, arrogant, self-centred intellectual – a "chip off the old block". During the course of my first career in banking, I became intellectually converted to the power of team-working and then emotionally converted.

Intellectual conversion

❏ I became intellectually converted to the power of effective team-working during the period 1982 to 1985. In 1982, I was appointed the Head Office trainer for the technical skills development of around 300 taxation staff, who worked in the 35 area offices of the financial services subsidiary of the bank.

❏ Training was delivered through a series of fortnightly courses, run on a residential basis from Head Office. I had experienced them all and they were absolutely dire – boring lectures delivered above our heads by experts who could not communicate, with occasional complex tests completed on an entirely individual basis, with hardly anyone achieving anywhere near a pass mark.

❏ I made three significant changes:

1. I introduced an initial case study to bring everyone up to speed, and a final case study to ensure that everyone had learnt all the material covered in the fortnight.

2. I deployed the learning cycle – tell, show, do and review, i.e. Progressive input of material, examples, testing knowledge and reviewing outcomes.

3. Testing was carried out on a group basis. In fact, from the moment the delegates arrived, they were put into and stayed in the same group of 5 or 6.

❏ As regards team selection, we had limited information to go on, but I made sure there was a mix of genders and cultural backgrounds, and separated out the very timid and the smart Alecs. A smart Alec is a "conceited know-it-all" – an individual who seeks to impress everyone with his intellectual prowess and prove his intellectual superiority. As mentioned, I was brought up to be a smart Alec.

❏ I also used rotating spokespersons. Two enormous bonuses were that the timid became much more confident, as they were

15

reporting back their group's answers rather than their own individual efforts, and the smart Alecs became treasured assets of the group.

❑ The results were spectacular. On the final Thursday on all the programmes, I handed out, at 9 a.m., the concluding case study to the three now high-performing teams. I went back to work on other matters until 4 pm. I then returned to the lecture room to receive the answers. As the marks did not fall below 95%, the next hour could be devoted to productive discussion and discovery.

❑ External evidence of success was the fact that the Area Managers were so delighted with the increased effectiveness and productivity of their taxation staff that my boss, the Head of Training, gained an early and unexpected promotion to Head of Personnel.

Emotional conversion

❑ I became emotionally converted to the power of effective team-working when I attended the one month's General Management Development programme in 1986, run by Ashridge Business College.

❑ On that programme, and on every other development programme I have attended, the lecturers paid very little attention to group dynamics.

❑ As a result, task excellence is denied, as the groups rarely get beyond the "storming" stage of team development, i.e. individualism is accentuated. The result is individuals vie for the leadership of the group, or sub-groups form and compete with each other, or an individual drops out, or all three. Generally speaking, there is maximum heat and minimum light.

❑ Now the climax to the programme was a highly competitive 3-day business simulation, where we were split into groups and stayed in those groups throughout.

❑ Although my ability to build any group into an effective team within 4 hours was over 8 years into the future, I had learnt enough from my experience as a technical skills trainer to build my group into a high-performing team within the 3 days.

❑ The determinant of victory was something called the Z coefficient, a complex combination of financial measures of success.

❑ My team won with the highest Z score by far since records began. A score of 1 represented a "going concern". The previous highest score had been 2.7. Our score was 5.6. The simulation had been running for many years.

❑ This was not the result of any individual's superior ability, but was produced by the creative and decision-making synergy that all high-performing teams deliver.

❑ Whilst the tutors did not believe the results and vainly tried to prove our team had cheated, my fellow delegates, 26 in number, knew the truth of the matter.

❑ I was the last to join the ante-chamber, where drinks were being served before the course dinner. When I entered, I received a prolonged round of applause from all my peers. The tutors kept their hands to themselves.

❑ It was an emotional high. Not only had I become the treasured asset of all my team-members, who were ecstatic to be part of a record smashing unit, but, for the first time in my life, I had gained the respect and admiration of all my peers.

CAREER AS A DEVELOPMENT CONSULTANT

❑ I joined Sundridge Park Management Centre in 1990 and focused my energies on researching into and thinking about how I could accelerate the production of a high-performing team.

❏ By the end of 1993, I had produced the recipe to enable a high-performing team to be built from any group in four hours. It is necessarily unique – my USP.

WHY THE RECIPE IS UNIQUE

There are three reasons:

1. Reading a critical research finding.
2. Developing a powerful creative thinking technique.
3. Overturning conventional wisdom.

1. READING A CRITICAL RESEARCH FINDING

❏ A.J Romiszowski wrote a book in 1984 entitled, 'Producing instructional systems – lesson planning for individualised and group learning activities.' He pointed out that the following benefits accrued to the individual, when working in an effective group.

Satisfies a social necessity

"Human beings are by nature sociable. Many aspects of modern life tend to diminish the opportunities for group interaction. (Effective) group work develops social skills, such as co-operation and strengthens social values."

Promotes intellectual development

"According to Piaget, rational thought (as opposed to superstitious or 'magical' thought) only develops when individuals meet in groups".

Humanises the teacher learner relationship

"The substitution of authoritarian teaching by the orientation of study in the group situation leads to greater interest and motivation on the part of the learners."

Promotes the development of personality

"The group is the appropriate environment for the personal development of the individual. Personality growth is largely the result of interaction between the individual and the group. According to Piaget, it is the result of co-operation. Thus we may argue that group work is truly individualising."

Promotes creativity

"The spirit engendered in group learning as a result of discussion, interchange and collaboration breaks down conventions, mental inertia and other barriers to innovative thinking."

❑ Once I discovered this finding, I realised that, if I could develop processes and tasks that produced the above beneficial outcomes, I would be able to create a high-performing team much more rapidly that I had been able to, when in a state of relative ignorance.

❑ As a starting point, I had already recognised that a positive environment and social behaviours could be created very rapidly. When I was in my last position at the bank as their first group strategic planning manager, I was asked to facilitate 11 peer group meetings, varying from secretaries to the senior management team in the department where I worked.

❑ The purpose was to review the findings of a staff attitude survey and come up with solutions for the department. At every meeting, within 10 minutes, I had created a positive environment with the appropriate behaviours – so that each meeting was an outstanding success. (Full details are set out in "Succeed as a Leader" in chapter 6, "Run a Successful Meeting".)

❑ What I also realised, when reflecting back on this experience, was that this outcome had been achieved irrelevant of the personalities of the individuals in the group, i.e. I would be able to build any group of individuals into an effective team.

2. DEVELOPING A POWERFUL CREATIVE THINKING TECHNIQUE

❏ I became a certified practitioner in the Ned Herrmann Whole Brain Dominance Instrument (HBDI) in 1993. This is a simple and powerful model, from which I developed my change preference questionnaire.

❏ I would ask you to consider the 4 sets of activities in the table below.

LEFT BRAIN ("A" & "B")	RIGHT BRAIN ("C" & "D")
"A" brain: Logical Detached (LD) • Analyse • Evaluate • Be rational • Determine implications • Find answers	**"D" brain: Positive Creative (PC)** • Show imagination • Explore • Challenge • Question • Take risks
"B" brain: Cautious Control (CC) • Resist • React • Play safe • Be organised • Show caution	**"C" brain: People Focused (PF)** • Accept • Share • Support • Care • Show sensitivity

❏ Make a decision for each set of activities, taken "as a whole" or "in the round" as to whether you:
  • Have a very strong preference (give yourself a score of 1+)
  • Have a clear preference (score of 1)
  • Would use them, are "OK" with them (score of 2)
  • Would avoid them (score of 3)

❑ By going through the alphabet in order, you have produced your change preference profile, e.g. Mine is (1,2,1,1+). I am 40% left-brained and 60% right-brained.

❑ What I also realised is that left-brained people use the opposite language to right-brained people for the same concept, e.g. the left-brained words *boss, manager, control, mission, training* as compared to the right-brained words *facilitator, leader, empower, vision, development.*

❑ Often organisations, without conscious awareness of the reasons, will use a combination of words, one that appeals to left-brained people and one that appeals to right-brained people, so as to appeal to both types. Examples would be *change management* and *New Labour.*

❑ As a result of all this discovery:

1. I realised that, to build a team rapidly, I needed to use whole-brained learning, i.e. combine the logical and process-driven thinking and behaviours that lie on the left side of the brain with the intuitive and innovative thinking and behaviours of the right side of the brain in a powerful integrated way.

2. I developed a creative thinking technique that, within less than an hour, enabled every group to produce creative synergy and every individual to acknowledge that truth as fact. The name of the technique is the *Group Discovery Technique (GDT).*

3. OVERTURNING CONVENTIONAL WISDOM

There are two areas where I overturned conventional wisdom:

1. Exclusive focus on the individual.
2. Misunderstanding the "storming" stage of team development.

1. Exclusive focus on the individual

❑ There is a remarkable and universal emphasis on individualism by experts on teams both in the UK and the US. It is understandable, given the individualistic cultures of both nations, but means that all these experts are incapable of producing the recipe. I will illustrate this reality by looking at Belbin, who has produced by far the most widely used team role questionnaire.

❑ To be seen as "scientifically" valid research, Belbin limited himself to an observer role only. This would have been quite frustrating, as most of the groups he observed would have been locked into the "storming" stage of team development.

❑ Eventually, one team would have reached the performance level, because it happened to contain individuals who collectively covered all the work functions – researching, applying specialist knowledge, co-ordinating, controlling, innovating, evaluating, supporting, implementing, completing.

❑ With the independent and individualistic focus, Belbin and all the other "experts" were incapable of stepping back at this stage to consider what processes could be put in place to ensure any group developed the ability to complete all the necessary work functions and hence get to high performance rapidly.

❑ Necessarily, the work functions were individualised and the questionnaire produced to identify individual strengths and weaknesses, i.e.

- *Specialist* : provides expert knowledge and skills in key areas.
- *Resource Investigator*: focuses on obtaining all the necessary resources.
- *Co-ordinator*: co-ordinates the team's efforts.
- *Shaper* : provides direction and focus.
- *Plant* : comes up with the ideas.
- *Team Worker* : cares for individuals and the team.

- *Monitor-Evaluator* : evaluates ideas and make sure the team stays on track.
- *Implementer*: focuses on driving the task through to completion – the plan is turned into action.
- *Completer-Finisher* : pays attention to detail and ensures the project is completed on time.

❑ Specifically, the personalisation of team functions denies any chance of producing creative synergy. Everyone turns to the individual with the highest score in "plant" and says: "You give us the ideas."

❑ Critically, the accentuation of individual difference inevitably pulls the team apart and denies the ability ever to produce an effective team at all, never mind rapidly.

- "I am a 'plant'. I am the ideas man, so I come up with all the ideas. Everyone else hates me, but I love myself."

- "I am a 'team worker'. I always make the tea. No-one ever listens to me. I spend all my time stopping the two 'shapers' killing each other."

- "I am a 'shaper'. I tell everyone what to do. I bully them all into submission. I know everyone hates me. Deep down, I want to be loved. Still, I quite like being the "big boss" and crushing everyone around me.

- "I am a 'monitor-evaluator'. Everyone hates me, but I simply cannot help playing to my strengths. I just get so much joy and personal satisfaction from killing every project stone dead."

- "I am the 'specialist' or knowledge expert. Of course, I always speak in gobbledygook and never share my expertise. Otherwise, I would no longer be indispensible and a superior human being."

- "I am a 'resource investigator". I avoid the team like the plague. I spend all my time networking like mad and bombarding the team with mountains of information, most of which is completely useless."

- "I am an 'implementer'. I am the task driver. I focus on the task, task, and task. Why is Harriet blubbing in the corner? Never mind – task, task, task. It is my life and I love it."

- "I am the "completer-finisher". I get the job done. I am a details person. The devil is in the detail and I make a very good devil. I nag, nag, nag, nag and nag. Persistence pays. I always get my own way. I may not be popular – but who cares? Nothing beats a good nag." (Or a good nagger does nothing but beat.)

2. Misunderstanding the "storming" stage of team development

❑ This is extremely commonplace and denies the ability to create a high-performing team. The classic example for me was about fifteen years ago now, when I was on a sales programme run by the sales director. There was a session on team-building and the director had covered the four stages of team development – forming, storming, norming, performing.

Author's note:

The "fact" that there are four stages of team development is another myth, exploded in chapter 7, "Break free from 'Received Wisdom'."

❑ He then proceeded to tell us all that you had to have "blood on the carpet" before you could build a high performing team, i.e. you had to enter a storming stage (where individualism was at its peak) and then resolve all the personality and ego clashes (produce lots of blood) before you could move on. If that happens, you can almost guarantee that the team will never perform and, at some stage, break up completely in a barrage of personal criticism and repeated poor performance.

❏ I can understand where the guy was coming from. Almost all people in the work-place spend a lot of time in the storming stage and never experience effective team-working. If they do, because some individual or process takes them out of storming into high performance, then they will believe that storming was a necessary evil or, in the case of the sales director, who was a very strong shaper (i.e. control freak), a necessary pleasure.

❏ There has not been a single drop of blood spilt in the four hours where I have helped create a high performing team (and, as mentioned, I have helped create over 1000 such teams).

❏ Now that does not mean to say that there is no storming stage or level. Once you have built a high-performing team, then the team will face many changes that could push it down to storming, e.g. change in team-member, additional member joining, existing member leaving, poor performance by an individual team-member and so on – internal or endogenous events. There are also external triggers or exogenous shocks like a sudden moving of the goal-posts by the boss or client and so on – see chapter 8, "Create Growth from Change".

❏ However, if all the team members know, in advance, all the triggers and all the strategies to deal with them, then the stay in storming is very brief, quickly cut short and high performance rapidly restored – see chapter 8 for details of those strategies.

❏ Finally, feedback given in the storming stage is negative and personally destructive, i.e. reduces confidence and self-esteem. Feedback, when the team has performed well and everyone has high-self esteem and confidence, is very constructive – see chapter 9, "Manage effective feedback".

HOW THE OBJECTIVE IS ACHIEVED FOR YOU

The objective is achieved by:

❑ Setting out in chapter 1 a number of tools and techniques that help you cope with the stresses and strains of life more effectively. Specifically, we look at how you can:

- Become *"cool, calm and collected"* à la Barack Obama.
- Use the *"cool" pause* to ensure you react calmly when provoked.
- Deploy the *quieting response* before entering an environment you consider will be stressful for you.
- Use *reflective listening,* when a TOP (**T**he **O**ther **P**arty in a relationship) is angry with you because you have made some mistake (in their eyes) that has caused them grief. Reflective listening ensures that the TOP thinks of you much more positively than was conceivable at the angry start, and avoids you having to justify or even acknowledge the "mistake".
- Uncover a *magical moment* from your past and then *create a circle of confidence* so that you can recall it in all its power and glory, whenever you so desire.
- Build self-confidence and self-esteem by creating your *affirmative statements*. These enable you to recognise how skilful and effective you are.

Author's note:

- They are provided as a menu from which you can pick and choose as you see fit.

- A key point is that you need to be fully confident that you will perform brilliantly on the day. Some or all of these tools and techniques will help.

❑ Advising you exactly what you should know and do before you run your on-site workshop. This is covered in chapter 2, "Prepare to Succeed".

❑ Setting out the recipe in detail – providing all the whats, whys, hows and whens. This is covered in chapter 3, "Create the Right Environment", chapter 4, "Promote Group Discovery", and chapter 5, "Harness the Power of Process".

❑ Producing a summary plan in chapter 6, "Recipe for action".

❑ Providing the information that you will require before running your team-building session, i.e.

- Looking in chapter 7 at all the areas where "received wisdom" denies the ability to create a high-performing team, including problems with stages of team development, phases, levels and lock-ins.

- Considering all the changes that impact on team performance and all the strategies to ensure a high level of performance is maintained over time – chapter 8, "Create Growth from Change".

- Setting out in Chapter 9, "Manage Effective Feedback", how to run a team-feedback session that guarantees each individual will develop key strengths to a higher level and reduce the impact of or eliminate relevant weaknesses.

❑ This concludes the book as far as the individual manager is concerned.

❑ For those of you who are CEOs/Chairmen/Managing Directors, I set out in appendix 1, Project Omega for Organisations, how, once a group of RTBs (**R**apid **T**eam **B**uilders) has been produced, nearly every employee in your organisation will be working in a high-performing team by the end of the project, which takes only 3 months to complete. The end result is rapid effective cultural change and a leap in profitability for companies or the rapid achievement of key goals for non-profit making organisations.

❑ Appendix 11 , Project Omega for Education, sets out how, once a group of RTBs (**R**apid **T**eam **B**uilders), combining teachers and educational experts, has been produced, nearly every child in

State Education will be a member of a high-performing team, at the end of the project, which takes only a year to complete. This will make every politician's dream of producing a talent based economy come true, as well as giving us a national competitive edge in the global market-place.

To conclude, you will find that building your group(s) into a winning team will be a wonderful experience.

It was for me, and it will be for you.

Have fun

Rupert

1

Tools and Techniques

INTRODUCTION

I set out the following tools and techniques that enable you to:

☐ Become *"cool, calm and collected"*.
☐ Use the *"cool" pause*.
☐ Deploy the *quieting response*.
☐ Use reflective *listening*.
☐ Uncover a *magical moment* from your past.
☐ Create a *circle of confidence.*
☐ Produce your *affirmative statements*.

BECOME COOL, CALM AND COLLECTED

We start by looking at the three factors that contribute to effective communication. These are what we say, how we say it and our body language. The table below sets out what constitutes each factor and the percentage contribution to effective communication.

Factor	Description	% Contribution
What we say	Actual words used	7%
How we say it	Tone of voice – cold through to warm Inflexion – way the tone changes Pitch and emphasis Speech patterns – fast, slow, hesitant Use of pauses	38%
Our body language	Use of the eyes – the window to the soul Gestures Body posture	55%

KEY POINTS

❏ According to Iceberg communication theory, around 90% of our communication and hence behaviour is driven from our subconscious – the "hidden depths".

❏ So the words we actually use (a miserable 7%) may be perfectly harmless – excellent words indeed. However the recipient of our communication subconsciously listens to and interprets the meaning according to the highly significant 93% – "how we say the words" and "our body language". They then consciously react according to how their subconscious has received the message.

❏ The three main types of behaviour are:

- Aggressive behaviour.
- Assertive behaviour or "cool, calm and collected behaviour", to which (to be consistent with "Succeed in Life") we will refer to as "cool" behaviour.
- Passive behaviour.

❑ The table below sets out the 93% for each type of behaviour, separating out into:

- Voice
- Speech
- Eyes
- Face
- Body
- Feeling

	Passive	*Cool*	*Aggressive*
Voice	❑ Sometimes wobbly ❑ Tone may be singsong or whining ❑ Over-soft or over-warm ❑ Quiet, often drops away at the end	❑ Steady and firm ❑ Tone is middle range and warm ❑ Sincere and clear ❑ Not over-loud or quiet	❑ Very firm ❑ Tone is sarcastic, sometimes cold ❑ Hard and sharp ❑ Strident, often shouting, rise at end
Speech	❑ Hesitant and filled with pauses ❑ Sometimes jerks from fast to slow ❑ Frequent throat-clearing	❑ Fluent, few awkward pauses ❑ Emphasizes key words ❑ Steady, even pace	❑ Fluent, few awkward hesitancies ❑ Often abrupt, clipped ❑ Emphasizes blaming words, often fast
Eyes	❑ Evasive, looking down	❑ Firm but not a "stare" down	❑ Tries to stare down and dominate

31

Face	❑ "Ghost" smiles when expressing anger or being criticised ❑ Eyebrows raised in anticipation (e.g. of criticism) ❑ Quick changing features	❑ Smiles when pleased, frowns when angry, otherwise open. ❑ Features steady, not wobbling ❑ Jaw relaxed, not loose	❑ Smile can become awry, scowls when angry ❑ Eyebrows raised in amazement/ disbelief ❑ Jaw set firm, chin thrust forward
Body	❑ Hand-wringing ❑ Hunching shoulders ❑ Stepping back ❑ Arms crossed for protection ❑ Covering mouth with hand ❑ Nervous movements which detract (shrugs and shuffles)	❑ Open hand movements (inviting to speak) ❑ "Measured pace" hand movements ❑ Sits upright or relaxed (not slouching or cowering) ❑ Stands with head held up	❑ Finger pointing ❑ Fist thumping ❑ Sits upright or leans forward ❑ Stands upright "head in air" ❑ Strides around (impatiently) ❑ Arms crossed (unapproachable)
Feeling	❑ Guilty	❑ Confident	❑ Angry

KEY POINTS

As regards the verbal component, you combine "I" statements with the "broken record". Looking at each in turn:

"I" statements

When communicating assertively or "coolly", you use the first person, e.g. "I need you to get to work on time." You are not impersonal, "it would be very nice if you would get to work on time", nor should you lay the source of the request elsewhere, "the boss wants you to get to work on time", or "it is company policy that you get to work on time", or "according to your job description, you have to get to work on time".

The broken record

❑ The "broken record" means that you simply, in a calm, confident manner, i.e. coolly, repeat the particular "I" statement as many times as it takes, until you get the desired "Yes". You will always be effective provided you completely ignore any excuse or reason provided for the bad behaviour.

❑ It is another example of the power of subconscious psychological osmosis (SPO) – see note. The repetition of the same statement operates through TOP's subconscious to produce the conscious agreement: "Yes, I will get to work on time in future."

❑ Typically, three times does the trick – the power of 3. Only once, in my personal experience, did it take more – five times to be precise. (See *Succeed as a Parent – ensure your children are your friends for life* for the application of this approach to children).

Author's note:

I set out an extract from *Succeed as Leader – become the boss from heaven not hell* that explains subconscious psychological osmosis or SPO.

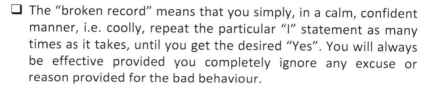

THE POWER OF SPO

From the moment we are born, a barrage of messages from a myriad of sources bombards our subconscious on a continuous basis.

If a given message is repeated sufficiently frequently in time and over time, then it seeps from our subconscious into our consciousness under the conscious radar, i.e. subconscious psychological osmosis or SPO. Eventually it can cause us to alter our behaviour from the historic norm or make a decision that accords with the message or form a new "fact" contained in the message.

We consciously believe that it is ourselves who have made up our own minds or deduced the new fact, as we have no conscious awareness of the "hidden truth".

An example would be Barack Obama. In the two years up to his election, his behaviour was consistently "cool, calm, and collected". This message was sufficiently reinforced that a subconscious mindset formed in the electorate that Barack was "cool, calm and collected".

When economic meltdown threatened, there was a marked shift towards Barack Obama as everyone knows you need a leader, who is "cool in a crisis".

Author's note:

❏ The three times rule generally holds for a single piece of information.
❏ Clearly if the message requires a new belief to come into place, then the repetition has to be much more frequent.
❏ Hence, of course, the power of "subliminal" advertising.

USE THE "COOL" PAUSE

❏ As soon as you have been provoked by a TOP (whether by e-mail, phone or face-face), take a deep breath, hold for a few seconds and then exhale right to the end of the breath, and hold for a few more seconds. This enables you, literally, to "clear your head" and remain or become "cool".

❏ It also allows TOP to calm down a bit (at the end of the phone or face-to-face) and begin to realise that he or she has gone over the top (pardon the pun). What you are doing is avoiding any "heat of the moment" comments, which one invariably one lives to regret.

❑ Put differently, what you are doing is avoiding a negative emotional response driven by your subconscious, which you cannot consciously control. You are retaining control of your communication and your behaviour.

DEPLOY THE QUIETING RESPONSE

❑ You use the quieting response:

- When you know that you will be entering an environment that is likely to cause you stress so that you can create a very relaxed and "quiet" state of mind – physically and mentally.
- After you have been in a stressful situation to eliminate the physical and thence mental tension.

❑ You tense four of the major muscle groups together and then relax to eliminate the physical and thence mental tension. Simultaneously:

- Clench both hands tightly into a fist.
- Tense your stomach muscles.
- Tense your neck by pressing your head back against an imaginary wall.
- Tense your jaw by clenching your teeth.

❑ Hold this position tightly for approximately eight to ten seconds. Then suddenly release it. Then relax:

- Drop your shoulders relaxing your neck.
- Your stomach muscles should flop and relax.
- Relax your jaw with your teeth slightly apart.

❑ At the same time as relaxing, put an "inward smiling face" on the side of your lips. Exhale deeply and hold your breath out. (If, as often the case, you are releasing stress after the event, and a particular individual X has caused that stress, then you have full permission to shout out loud at this juncture, if on your own, or say to yourself, if others are present, "Stuff X" or whatever form of terminology takes your fancy. If X happens to be present, then I suggest you keep the words used to yourself!)

❑ Keep this position for as long as possible. Then take a shallow breath only.

❑ With practice, the technique can be used without there being observable consequences to the untrained eye, especially as you can move from clenching each fist to pressing the fingers against the thumb tip on either hand and from then only pressing the fingers against the thumb tip on one (your preferred) hand.

❑ "Practice makes perfect" or, according to the Neuro-Linguistic Programming Society (NLP), repetition at least 20 times creates a new positive habit.

USE REFLECTIVE LISTENING

❑ This is an extraordinary powerful and effective technique. Whenever TOP is aggressive towards you for some perceived mistake you have made, use it. It is just as effective, whether the aggression occurs over the phone or face-to-face.

❑ Let us take an example. Your boss, John, dashes into your office and barks aggressively: "The deadline for your project paper was 12 noon. It is now 2 pm and I need it right away".

❑ John's communication contained a **fact** – that you had missed the agreed deadline; a **need** – that he had to have your project paper right and an **emotion** – anger towards you. Incidentally, all communications contain, at most, these three components.

❑ What we usually do, in reply, is to acknowledge our mistake (their fact), apologise for it, try to explain it away and then promise to correct it ASAP – meet their need. That approach generates a perception of incompetence in your boss's eyes. "Reflective listening" reverses this perception. You need to take three actions:

1. Stay "cool".
2. Eliminate TOP's emotion.
3. Meet the need.

Looking at each in turn:

1. Stay "cool"

☐ To avoid slipping into either aggression or passivity, when faced by an irrational emotional controller, you must maintain the "cool" state that will become your norm in the work-place – if you successfully demonstrate "cool behaviour" at least 20 times consecutively WITHOUT any lapse into aggressive or passive mode.

☐ To do so, straightaway deploy the "cool pause" or pauses.

2. Eliminate TOP's emotion

☐ Until you can return TOP back into a rational adult state, TOP will continue to be an irrational controller. So you have to address and **only** address the emotion first (and sometimes second, third, fourth and so on) until the aggressor has calmed down and returned to adulthood. Then and only then do you address the need.

☐ Even when people have recognised the need to address the emotional state first, unwittingly, they often add fuel to the flames, e.g. "I can see you are a little upset, John". To which comes the reply: "I am not a little upset, as you put it, Kate, I am very angry." The secret is never to understate the degree of emotion, but deliberately overstate it. "I can see that you are really furious with me, John, and I am sorry to have caused it" (or words to that effect). "I am not furious – just a bit annoyed," comes the reply.

☐ There is a subtle psychological process at play. When individuals are aggressive, they simply want you to do what they want done straightaway. They are itching to have a fight with you, and will be subconsciously driven to disagree with anything you say. When you understate the emotional intensity, they have to disagree and say: "I am very angry." Now, if some-body says out loud they are very angry, the need for street cred and the power of auto-suggestion mean they must become very angry. You pour fuel on the flames, and get severely burnt as a result.

❑ The converse, therefore, holds true. They automatically disagree with your statement that they are very furious, counter with the statement: "I am, actually, only a little bit annoyed."Then they start becoming only a little bit annoyed. This process is helped by the fact that, again subconsciously, they want to avoid the wrong label. Lots of bosses don't mind having a reputation of being a firm, authoritative leader. Few want the label of "Mr. or Mrs. Furious" in the company!

3. Meet the need

Once John is back to normal, you conclude with: "The final version of the paper will be on your desk by 3 pm."

Key points

❑ A key benefit of reflective listening is that, at no point, do you either acknowledge or apologise for the "mistake" (only for causing the emotion), and so you do not have to justify it.

❑ You leave TOP (in this case, your boss) with the memory of competence rather incompetence. If you had apologised for the mistake, you have admitted it and bosses, typically, don't like listening to a load of excuses or "whining". If you go the non-reflective listening route, you just confirm your incompetence in their eyes.

❑ Moreover, there always two sides to any "mistake". It may well be a "fact" for John that you have missed the deadline, i.e. made a mistake. However, there are "facts" for you, e.g. John endlessly dumps work on you, never provides proper briefings, and his deadlines are rather elastic – the work just sits on his desk day after day, i.e. three mistakes in your eyes.

❑ No, a great idea to use "reflective listening" to avoid heated discussion of "mistakes" and the reduction in quality of a relationship that is key to your career success.

❑ The reason why the technique is called "reflective listening" is because you **listen** to the emotion and **reflect** (and exaggerate) that back before addressing the need, and ignoring the "fact".

UNCOVER A MAGICAL MOMENT

We all have some magical memories of golden moments – when we experience elation, joy and a sense of wonderment. Walk back down the corridors of time to recall the most magical moment you have experienced to date.

CREATE A CIRCLE OF CONFIDENCE

❑ To create a circle of confidence, you need to do the following:

- Draw an imaginary circle in front of you.
- Take a deep breath.
- Step into the circle and relive the magical moment, dwell on it, rejoice in it – intensify the feelings, if you can.
- Step outside, letting go.
- Think of a code word that you will associate with that memory.
- Take a deep breath and step back in, adding the code word as you do. Relive the moment and come out of the imaginary circle.
- Repeat 7 times, always saying the code word to yourself when you step in.
- Take a break.
- Step into the circle and just say the code word.

❏ The memory and positive emotions should be triggered by the code word. If not, repeat until it is. You have created a state of mind, which fills you with confidence and joy and which you can use whenever you want to in the future by simply taking a deep breath, stepping into an imaginary circle, and repeating the code word.

PRODUCE YOUR AFFIRMATIVE STATEMENTS

❏ The way to do this is to produce **written,** what are called in the trade, "Affirmative Statements". This is best done with a TOP, where you have a relationship of mutual respect. A mutual process, a shared voyage of discovery, leads to better outcomes for both individuals.

❏ So, first of all, we deal with "Working with TOP" and then repeat the process, on the basis that you prefer to work alone. For those of you, who intend to work solo, it is helpful if you read "Working with TOP" first.

WORKING WITH TOP

❏ You and TOP both need a pen and paper. Let us assume that we start with you. TOP helps you by jogging your memory and ensuring that you dig out all your achievements and successes. This can be quite difficult, as we are all affected be cultural conditioning – the tendency for all our defects and flaws to be pointed out quite frequently, due to the prevailing "blame culture". TOP also acts as your scribe, leaving you free to think and speak.

❏ We now turn to the complete process whereby you (and then TOP) produce your affirmative statements. Then we will consider how you and TOP can use them to best effect.

The process

1. With TOP's help, you reflect on your past and think of (then state out loud and TOP writes down) any success – any achievement – you feel proud of, whether you perceive it as minor or major. Examples would be any achievement in the academic or sporting worlds; anything in your world of work from completing a major project to dealing with a difficult client; making an excellent presentation; any success in your social world from organising an event to hosting a successful dinner party; and any success in your private relationships – whether acts of kindness, cooking a TOP a nice meal, cheering TOP up when depressed and so on and so on. There is no upper limit to the number of your successes and achievements TOP writes down, but the minimum required is 10.

2. The second step is to consider each achievement in your ranking order of importance. When you consider the first, it is not very helpful for TOP simply to ask you the question: *"What are all the qualities and skills you displayed?"* What is a better way to yield the complete set of qualities and skills is for TOP to ask you to tell him or her (and TOP writes down) all the actions you took in time sequence to achieve that success. Then you look together at the process (set of activities carried out) as a whole, and distil all the qualities and skills demonstrated.

❑ Let us take an example. Not long ago, I persuaded a former work colleague/friend, Gary, that he should produce his affirmative statements. There was a bit of "trouble and strife" at home. Gary, who was a bit of an unregenerate when it came to the domestic side of things, had been "persuaded" that he should learn to cook. He had agreed, but was determined to learn for himself and not receive any "guidance" from his wife. He was very keen to "hit the decks running" and chose "garlic chicken" for his first attempt.

❑ It was an outstanding success. So, as TOP, I asked him to tell me exactly what was the process – the series of activities in time sequence – he had carried out. He told me that he had:

- Surfed the net and came across a recipe that he liked.

- Purchased all the ingredients, paying particular attention to best quality.

- Carefully prepared all the ingredients, including the garlic paste.

- Developed a time-plan, using the approximate timings provided, so that the meat and three veg would all be cooked at the same time.

- Boiled kettles and poured the boiling water into the 3 pans for the vegetables, well in advance of the time required, and kept the water just below simmering heat, so that he could bring the water back to the boil instantly, before putting in the vegetables according to the time plan.

- Adjusted the heat to ensure approximate timings became accurate ones, i.e. the vegetables and chicken in its sauce were all completed at the same time.

- Regularly tasted each component as it neared completion – to ensure the vegetables had the right "*bite*", the potatoes had just the right "*give*" when forked, and the chicken with its sauce was "*well done*".

❑ The qualities and skills that can be distilled from this sequence of activities were – seeking advice from an expert, organising, setting goals, planning, paying attention to detail, and showing flexibility in implementing plans.

❑ Once you and TOP have derived all the qualities and skills from your first success, you move on to the next achievement, and continue until you have produced a minimum of 20 different qualities and skills. You will find that, with each success, there will be some duplication of qualities and skills from previous successes, but also completely new ones.

❏ Next, you and TOP look at all your qualities and skills and produce three affirmative statements, each containing three connected qualities or skills. For example, Gary's were:

1. I am ascetic, resolute and disciplined.
2. I am calm, confident and kind.
3. I work hard, plan well and focus on results.

Author's note: The rule of 3 is used twice as that is the easiest way to remember and provides the most power, e.g. I came, I saw, I conquered.

❏ Once these have been produced, you reverse the process – help TOP produce his or her affirmative statements.

Effective use

❏ Now the thing about these affirmative statements is that they are statements of fact – not a wish list. "*I am calm, confident, and kind*" is much more powerful and effective than "*I would like to be calm, confident and kind.*" In the past, you (or TOP) have displayed all these qualities and skills.

❏ So what you should do is to write them down, learn them by heart and regularly repeat them to yourself. Waking up every morning and repeating them out loud from the written list a few times gets the day off to an excellent start. I know one individual, who has put them on a CD, and plays them to himself on the way to and from work.

❏ As you will appreciate, by regular repetition and reminder you, through SPO, are "bringing out the best in yourself."

❏ Finally, when you know you have a particular change to make or project to complete, you can develop affirmative statements that are specific to the requirements for success when making that change or completing that project – by looking back to the pool of qualities and skills you have developed, choosing those needed and writing specific affirmative statements.

WORKING ON YOUR OWN

You will need pen and paper. Then take the following steps:

1. List down at least 10 achievements or successes.

2. Taking each success in turn, starting with what you consider the most important, and set out the process, i.e. set of activities in time sequence you followed to achieve the success.

3. Looking at the process as whole, distil all the qualities and skills you displayed.

4. Continue with each success, until you have produced a minimum of 20 qualities or skills.

5. From the pool of 20+ qualities and skills, write down three affirmative statements, e.g. I am ascetic, resolute and disciplined, each containing three connected qualities and skills.

6. Learn them by heart and repeat them regularly to yourself.

$$\frac{\underline{\underline{\textbf{2}}}}{}$$

Prepare to Succeed

INTRODUCTION

Before you start the recipe, there are six pieces of information you need to know/actions you need to take:

1. Recognise the limitation in group size.
2. Act as a coordinator.
3. Believe in yourself.
4. Believe in your group members.
5. Read the book through.
6. Prepare to succeed.

1. RECOGNISE THE LIMITATION IN GROUP SIZE.

❑ You may have noticed that I have frequently referred in the introduction to an effective group rather than an effective team. This is deliberate. Many years ago, I was talking to the Managing Director of a multi-national travel services company. During the course of the conversation, he said to me: "I have a fantastic team". So, I said to him: "That's great, and how many are in your team?" To which he replied, "ten thousand" (the entire work-force).

❑ The point is that, if you want to create an effective team, there is a limitation on the numbers (including yourself) that comprise the unit. Of the 1000 groups I mentioned, the smallest group size was four and the largest group size was seven.

❑ The reason why we have a cut-off of four is that you need a critical mass of group members to produce the Romiszowski benefits.

❑ The reason for the cut-off of seven is because of what happens when you are part of an effective group. It is a wonderful, exhilarating and rewarding experience. Without consciously recognising it, your ego becomes suppressed as your needs are being met by the power of the group.

❑ Your focus becomes external rather than internal. You become very aware of other group members and want to help them. There is a limit to how many people we can become aware of at the same time. Again that that is true is not in doubt.   We look at the first case study – learning from my mistakes.

LEARNING FROM MY MISTAKES

This is the answer given to me by the Managing Partner of an international office of a Global Law Firm to the following question: "What had been the most recent challenges he had faced and what had he learnt from them?"

"Well, funny you should ask that as I have just finished being the lead partner in a big multimillion dollar, multi-jurisdictional transaction that lasted 9 months and involved 25 lawyers from a number of different offices working full-time. It was successful but it was a nightmare with enormous stress and 'blood on the carpet' on the way. I made two key mistakes.

First of all, I spent far too much time thinking and planning this vital transaction on my own. This meant that, when I called in the other partners, I controlled far too much and I pushed through decisions that backfired. I should have been an effective co-ordinator rather than an ineffective controller.

Secondly, we got all 25 lawyers together for a day. God that was awful – incredible heat and very little light. In hindsight, I should have started with a project steering group with me as co-ordinator and four other senior partners. Each of the partners should have been the co-ordinator of a sub-group of around 4 or 5 lawyers. Then we should have had a team-based strategic planning day, which would have created an effective strategy and action plans *and* the momentum to drive them through."

2. ACT AS A CO-ORDINATOR.

❑ I have just had some fascinating confirmation of both the need to act as a co-ordinator and keep the team size between 4 and 7. I listened recently to Paul Azinger, in a TV interview, explain why the US won the Ryder Cup in 2008.

❑ The US were significant underdogs as they had lost the four previous encounters. The UK team was lead by Nick Faldo, a strange choice in that he was noted as a being a self-centred individualistic type of person – but then the UK is not big on teams, as covered in the introduction.

❑ What Paul Azinger did was to split the 12 players into 3 pods of four. He had 3 lieutenants, as compared to Nick Faldo's one, for which he was criticised as showing weak leadership. He said that he thought it had showed strong leadership as he trusted them, they had clear roles and they got on well with the players.

❑ Paul Azinger also said that he picked the pairings on the basis of like personalities rather than like games, i.e. people who got on well with each other rather than people who played golf in a similar way.

❑ In short, a handsome victory was achieved, reversing the underdog status because:
1. Paul was a co-ordinator of his team rather than a "command and control" leader with no team.
2. His lieutenants' key role was also co-ordinating/coaching – helping to build each of the 3 pods into high-performing units, in which they were successful.

❑ So the team approach enabled the US to exceed all expectations, as the American golfers played, "out of their skins". The individualistic approach meant that the European golfers fell below what was expected of them, given their overall superior position in the individual rankings. Too many did not: "step up to the plate".

❑ It is, of course, the same in any sport with large team numbers. You can have team spirit in rugby, football and cricket (taking but three examples) , but, to have effective team-working, you need to break the team down into units, e.g. defensive/midfield/attacking for football and not try the impossible, i.e. to create effective team-working from the full group rather than the smaller units.

❑ Finishing on a footballing note, when the attacking unit has become an effective team, then all the individuals focus on maximising the probability that a shot on goal will produce a goal. Hence the brilliant passing to the player who can "tap in" rather than endless low probability scoring shots by players, ignoring the unmarked player screaming for the pass, concentrating on individual glory (and to be fair, sometimes, job survival) at the expense of team success.

3. BELIEVE IN YOURSELF

❑ You will be the only one of your team to have read this book. Knowledge gives you power and increases self-belief. The very act of reading this book – developing your awareness and understanding – will increase your confidence.

❑ You can also select from the tools and techniques from the first chapter and practise whichever you choose before the big day, so that you know that you will be successful.

4. BELIEVE IN YOUR GROUP MEMBERS

❑ In a research experiment into the impact of expectations on results, around 60 young school children of average ability were split into three equal groups. Each group was taught by a different teacher, none of whom had met the children before. Let us call the teachers A, B and C. The A teacher was told that she was receiving bright, able, committed children; the B teacher was told that she was receiving average, run-of-the-mill kids and the C teacher was told that she was getting a bunch of below average, rude and rebellious children – the "dross".

❑ Six months later, all the children in each of the three groups were performing and behaving exactly according to the expectations given to each teacher.

❑ If you have faith in the potential of all your group members, suspend your initial judgements formed from working with them on an individual basis and rigorously avoid the display of any favouritism, each group member will have confidence in themselves, derived from the confidence you show in them and you will be able to create a high-performing team.

5. READ THE BOOK THROUGH

It is important that you read beyond the chapters that cover the recipe as you will need to know how to handle changes that will affect your team and how to run an effective feedback session.

PREPARE TO SUCCEED

❑ You need to get a date in diaries for an on-site half-day for all the team-members. All they need to know is that the objective of the half-day is to improve team-working, which could, of course, be very good to start with. You will need a separate meeting room with table and chairs, one flip-chart, plenty of flip-chart pens and spare flip-chart paper.

❑ You will also need blue tack or masking tape to hang your output around the walls. There should be no individual pieces of paper or individual writing, apart from you as the co-ordinator or any designated scribe during the actual event.

❑ There will some material you will want to write up on the flip-chart in advance or hand-out. This will be clearly indicated in the summary plan that forms chapter 6. Coffee, tea and so on should be on tap and, built into the process plan, is a fifteen minute break.

❑ All mobiles should be turned off and there should be no external interruptions. It is absolutely essential that the entire group are together (body and soul) throughout the half day – apart from the official break.

❑ If you don't think your culture permits that, then I would recommend going off-site. If you do decide to do that, it would be a good idea to relax together over a nice lunch before returning to the office. In fact, it would be a good idea, though not essential, to go for lunch afterwards – have a relaxing environment to reflect together and unwind – even if you do carry out the half-day on site.

❑ Of course, diary commitments may be such that you are holding the half-day in the afternoon, in which case a drink before going your separate ways could take place.

❑ You will be the best judge of location and whether it would help to have an informal continuation of the event.

❑ Finally, it may be that your team is geographically dispersed – what is termed a "virtual" team. In this case, it would make sense to have a special event, where you meet at some convenient hotel or conference centre.

    • The costs of travel and accommodation will be more than offset by the value you will gain from building your virtual team into a real team and the subsequent sharp upward movement in productivity and efficiency.

- You may want to take the opportunity to have a full day. Once you have read the book, you will be able to choose how the extra time can best be spent.

- If you do this, please ensure that any socialising takes place after the event and not before. I have run quite a number of team-building/strategy events, e.g. For an entire department including junior staff and PAs, for all the executives and senior managers of a particular company, for functional departments, business areas and so on.

- Typically, they start on a Friday or a Saturday and have a half-day on the Saturday or Sunday. Invariably the half day is a waste of time, as the socialising has been too long and too liquid.

- I can recall one such event where I turned up promptly at 9 a.m. I was alone apart from the in-house administrator. People started drifting in from 9.25 onwards. The most senior executive, who was the sponsor of the event, turned up at 11 a.m. Needless to say little was done and the little that was done was not done well.

- It was scheduled to finish at 1 p.m., and actually finished at 12 p.m. It started with a bang and ended with a whimper.

- Yours should start with a bang and end with a firework display.

3

Create the Right Environment

INTRODUCTION

In this third chapter, we cover the first of the three key exercises. Specifically we look at:

- ❑ What you do.
- ❑ Why you do it.
- ❑ Case study of success.
- ❑ How you do it.
- ❑ How you ensure momentum is maintained.

WHAT YOU DO

❑ You tell the group, having confirmed the purpose of the morning/afternoon, that: "In this first exercise we are going to share from our experiences of working in an effective team (any team – work, school project, sports, social, whatever – in our past) what were all the *attitudes* we adopted and *actions* we took when we were in that team."

❑ The above does not have to all be written down. It is critically important that, throughout, you use the style and approach with which you are comfortable.

❑ You could simply write on the flip-chart, "Attitudes and "Actions" or add other key words – like "Any Team", "Sharing", "Experience".

❑ The reason is that I use "any team" is because many people may not have experienced a really bonded and effective group in the work-place (for the reasons given in the introduction) but most have outside work.

WHY YOU DO IT

❑ You are starting at the end, as I did when I built my team at Ashridge to achieve such spectacular success, i.e. you are getting everyone at the start of the team-building process to commit to the behaviours individuals exhibit at the end, when operating in successful or high-performing teams.

❑ You are focussing on the critical determinant of success, i.e. how we behave towards to each other, what is often termed the "culture", in which we operate.

❑ You are basing discovery on sharing – a key feature of any effective team.

❑ You are sharing from experience, rather than giving theoretical input. Recapturing a positive experience is much more powerful for the individual than any theoretical input.

❑ By starting at the end, you ensure that you will reach the end rapidly (more or less straightaway).

❑ The repetition and reinforcement of the right behaviours over a four hour period means that they become embedded.

CASE STUDY OF SUCCESS

FROM TEARS TO HAPPINESS

About a decade ago now, I was running a management development programme that was split into two modules, about three or four months apart.

The climax of the first module, when all the groups had become effective teams and so were willing to open up to each other, was for each team-member to share their deepest concerns and we would use the power of the team to try to resolve them.

It will come as no surprise to you that it is problems in relationships that universally cause the most stress and headaches for the individual, rather than the work itself.

Janice, we will call her, had a dual role. She was a PA in a pod system but also the manager of the pod, i.e. had 5 PAs to look after.

Penny had lost her best mate as the result of a secretarial review a few months earlier and had become demotivated and isolated from the rest of the team. Her performance was variable and she behaved irrationally a lot of the time – aggressive to passive and back again.

The whole team was affected. Janice had tried to adopt a calm considerate approach and had had quite a number of 1-on-1s with Penny which got nowhere. Either Janice was in danger of losing her own cool at the aggressive response or was faced with a woman weeping uncontrollably.

She had contemplated involving HR and starting the disciplinary process, but knew that, if she did, she would get a black mark for failing to be a competent manager. She was at her wits' end.

As a result of the group's input, Janice decided to stop "knocking her head against the Penny brick wall" and carry out the attitudes and actions exercise that she had done at the beginning of the programme – for the whole team.

She did and reported back at the beginning of the second module. Not total success, but a giant leap forward. Penny was now part of the team, who were performing much better as a unit. Penny still had occasional mood swings but these were tolerated by the team. Penny's overall performance had gone up considerably.

From Penny's point of view, she was part of a process or exercise that included everyone – not an individual being "picked on". This is, of course, the power of a team approach.

No individual blame produces maximum team gain.

HOW DO YOU DO IT

❑ This may seem a strange question, but it isn't. As coordinator, you will be the focus of attention, as you will be the scribe and writing the answers of the group on the flip chart. You will be contributing, but your key role is to ask questions.

❑ You see, what happens is that groups tend to find it easier to come up with an attitude than an action. For instance, some-one might say: "show each other respect". Great, that is an excellent attitude to have and is one that is the hall-mark of effective teams, i.e. mutual respect.

❑ It is actions that determine outcomes. So, you may need to ask the group. "Excellent – but how do we show respect?" Some-one will answer: "We need to listen to each other".

❑ It is much easier, when some-one is not listening, for some-one else to say (in a warm tone of voice). "We all agreed that we would listen to each other – so could you please listen to me". "Sorry, of course I will".

❑ It is much tougher for the individual to take an "attack" on an attitude that they are no longer displaying, e.g. "You are not showing me respect" or, in modern parlance, "You are dissing me."

❑ Whenever I have facilitated this exercise, I have simply accepted the presentations made by the different groups, unless there is a vital action missing.

❑ In the work-books, we put together the following template:

Attitudes	Actions
Trust	Sharing
Honesty	Creating safe, confidential environment
Respect	Listening
Interest	Staying focused and contributing
Humility	Trying out other's ideas
Openness	Altering opinions
Support	Praising and encouraging
Co-operation	Suppressing ego
Challenge	Questioning
Reflection	Planning

❑ You and your group may come up with more or less. There is no need to have a perfect correlation with one attitude producing one action. It is a process that can evolve. You can add or subtract to the list as the result of experience.

❑ As long as key elements are there, that is fine. Generally speaking, groups tend to have one important omission and make one mistake.

OMISSION

❑ The omission tends to be "challenge". I can understand that, as "challenge" is a confrontational word – the only confrontational attitude in this particular list.

❑ When I am the facilitator, then I don't mention the word "challenge". What I say is that it would a good idea if they added to the list of actions – that they should ask questions, as that is the key to learning and discovery.

MISTAKE

Many, many groups either put up that they should provide "constructive criticism" or the gentler "politically correct" phrase "give feedback". This is an absolute no no. This is proved in the next case study – learning from experience

LEARNING FROM EXPERIENCE

In 1985, I attended a two week team-building programme run for bank staff. I decided that I would not be my normal arrogant intellectual self, but, drawing from the list on the previous page, would show respect, humility, support and co-operate. In terms of actions, "listen, try out other's ideas, praise and encourage, and suppress ego".

I was successful, in that our team was the only team of the three that made it to a cohesive, high-performing unit.

On the final Thursday afternoon, we were told by our tutors to go to our syndicate rooms and write down everything we liked and disliked about our fellow team-members, and distribute our sheets of paper around.

We decided to keep the negatives to one and accentuate all the positives and so came out psychologically unscathed.

However, there was one individual, we will call Richard, who was a member of one of the other groups, who never made it the "commitment" level.

Now, during the fortnight, every team-member had had the opportunity to be the leader of one of the many projects we carried out.

Richard thought that he was a brilliant leader – but had, in fact, been useless – basically been the "big boss" – not listening to anyone, ignoring others' ideas and ordering people about. So, having been given permission by these team-destroying tutors, they all wrote this down in great detail and handed it to the poor unfortunate.

Most of us have gaps between our conscious self-image and view of ourselves (accentuating the positive) and the whole truth. We tend to have the darker side of our natures lurking in our subconscious as negative forces that drive action without conscious control or recognition of bad behaviour. If you like, many of us believe ourselves consciously to be Dr Jekylls and not recognise our hidden My Hydes.

Now, if Richard had had but a single piece of paper from one individual saying, "you are a very Hydeous", he would have rejected it out right (too much damage to conscious self-image and confidence levels) and "shot the messenger" – in fact, accused the messenger of the same faults, he could not see in himself.

Poor Richard had 6 other people simultaneously telling him that he was the opposite of what he believed himself to be. He simply could not handle it. He got very drunk indeed, damaged some furniture and then physically assaulted a member from another training programme being run at the Centre. He was subsequently "let go".

HOW YOU ENSURE MOMENTUM IS MAINTAINED

❑ The key question you ask your group is: "Well, that's great. We have agreed all the attitudes we are going to adopt and actions take, but how do we ensure that we will actually carry them out?"

❑ At the end of the discussion, the answer will pop out, if necessary, after a gentle bit of steering from yourself: "Anyone in the group is given permission by all the other members to point out any breach of the rules by any member."

❑ This is an extra-ordinarily effective way of overcoming the drawbacks of and clashes between different personality types, without ever referring to them.

❑ Some people are not very good listeners. They genuinely commit to listening. If they demonstrably fail to listen and some-one with a positive tone of voice and genuinely supportively points that out, they accept it without demur and with no negative feelings toward the other person.

❑ They have unintentionally broken something they want to do. They are annoyed with themselves and not the other person.

❑ What also happens, quite remarkably, is that, because the 4 hour process ensures continuation of all the positive behaviours, they start catching themselves out before they are caught up. "Oh! God, that's my ego speaking" or "I have stopped listening".

❑ As regards timings, this session takes approximately half an hour. So the clock has moved from 09.00 to 09.30.

4

Promote Group Discovery

INTRODUCTION

❑ The Group Discovery Technique (GDT) is the means by which each individual in the group discovers that the group can produce more and better ideas than any individual. This, as mentioned earlier, is called creative synergy.

❑ For it to be successful you follow a simple process, i.e. a set of rules/activities in a time sequence, and continue to follow the behaviours to which each individual is now committed.

❑ It is extraordinarily powerful because it converts the most cynical and sceptical individual to the fact that the team is more effective than the individual.

❑ All of you will have heard of the word "brainstorming". There are two drawbacks to "brainstorming".

1. Terminology.
2. Application in real life.

1. TERMINOLOGY

Brainstorming is a right-brained word that subconsciously irritates left-brained people. Indeed, I ran a workshop recently, building a group of four comic actors into a team using the recipe, and none of them liked the word – and they are all right-brained!

2. APPLICATION IN REAL LIFE

❏ When I am promoting discovery of the first two rules of GDT, I ask the groups if they have ever been in a team-meeting, where they have been asked to contribute ideas as part of a "brainstorming session". A universal "Yes".

❏ I then ask what happens in real life. Invariably some-one will say that their idea was ridiculed or criticised.

❏ I then ask what the consequence of that criticism is. The answer is that they stop contributing their ideas.

❏ I then ask what the outcome of this "brainstorming session" is. The reply is "the one right answer."

❏ I then ask who provides "the one right answer". The answer is the BOSS.

I now turn to:

❏ The four rules of GDT.
❏ Testing.
❏ The outcomes produced.
❏ Ensuring you stay true to your own style.
❏ Creative thinking scenarios.

THE FOUR RULES OF GDT

1. Separate out exploration from evaluation.
2. Stamp on criticism.
3. Help develop other's ideas.
4. Be creative on assumptions.

1. SEPARATE OUT EXPLORATION FROM EVALUATION

❑ You will come to the evaluation stage when you are applying the process to progress your key strategic issue in the next step.

❑ When you apply and prove the power of GDT in the testing phase in this step, remember that there will be no evaluation – you will stay in exploration or creative mode.

Author's note:

- You will find that, in the testing phase, you will get a whole range of answers (all of them "right answers") and, in the example provided before testing, the group produced a quantum leap, as an answer.

- There was no formal evaluation phase because the next rule, "Stamp on Criticism", was rigorously upheld.

- The point is, when you are in purely creative mode, you don't know where it will lead you – the nature and the beauty of exploration only.

2. STAMP ON CRITICISM

This is critical to avoid the "one right answer". It is also critically important to stamp on non-verbal as well as verbal criticism. As body language contributes 55% to effective communication, a look to the ceiling or a shrug of the shoulders are just as effective as a critical comment with a harsh tone of voice.

3. HELP DEVELOP OTHERS' IDEAS

❑ Synergy is not achieved by pooling individual suggestions, but by building on them through open questions, so that there is a flow of ideas and, hence, potential solutions. The individual should think of their idea as a gift to the group to be changed from silver into gold – not as something that must be jealously guarded and protected: *"Because it's my idea, not yours. My idea is bigger than yours."*

❑ I provide an example of the first three rules in action – the Alaskan Electricity Company:

ALASKAN ELECTRICITY COMPANY

The Alaskan Electricity Company faced terrible problems in the 1970s. It managed over 1000 miles of over ground telegraph poles, supplying electricity to a sparse and widely scattered population in very hostile weather conditions.

As a result of the terrible weather, ice and snow gathered on the overhead cables, which frequently snapped under the weight. Teams of men had to travel miles and miles to repair these cables. The costs of such operations exhausted all their profits.

The company solved the problem through a group of people questioning effectively and following the three rules. These are the questions:

- Why not shake the poles?
- How do we shake the poles?
- Why not use polar bears?
- How do we motivate the bears to shake the poles?
- Why not put meat on top of the poles?
- How do we get meat on top of the poles?
- Why not use a helicopter?
- Why not forget about the bears and use the whirring blades of the helicopter to get rid of the snow and ice, before it forms?

And that is what the Alaskan Electricity Company did – with considerable cost saving. Prevention was cheaper than cure.

Key points

☐ There was a logical connection between the open, exploring "how" question and the actual idea or suggestion prefaced by "why not". Logical, practical people often label themselves as not being very creative. Provided you suspend judgement and do not criticise yourself, logical people can be extremely creative.

☐ Indeed, if you accept my definition of intuition as the "subconscious learning from experience that rests in the subconscious", then I would argue that learning is a processing of the experience, i.e. thinking logically with connected steps as in the above. The subconscious brain obeys the first two rules. This is why, if we sleep on a problem, the subconscious brain may solve it for us.

☐ If you practise this approach to creative problem-solving (on your own as an individual), you will become more intuitive and a quantum leaper.

☐ Clearly criticism would have killed the solution stone dead. Those who criticise always have to give a reason. So we would have had comments along the lines of:

- "Why not shake the poles?" – "What a stupid impractical idea?"

- "Why not use polar bears?" – "How ridiculous. I have done my research and there are 3 million poles and 650 polar bears."

- "Why not put meat on top of the poles?" – "How stupid can you get? The polar bears would smash the wires in the attempt to get the meat."

☐ There was a clear "helping others' ideas", which is why a very neat solution emerged so quickly. The group achieved a quantum leap, and, as mentioned before, so can you individually.

❑ The final point is that this was a specific, concrete problem and, in this case, GDT produced an excellent solution achieved by purely using open questions.

❑ When you are addressing your strategic issue in the next session, GDT will produce a whole range of ideas, which the group will need to evaluate as part of the process. Clearly there can be a neat solution to the specific "snow and ice problem" but a range of "answers" to an issue like "changing culture effectively" – the most important of which can be implemented through the appropriate projects.

4. BE CREATIVE ON ASSUMPTIONS

We look at:

❑ The reason for the rule
❑ Application of the rule

Reason for the rule

❑ Daily life requires that we make assumptions. However, trainers often point that, if we ASSUME, we are making an "ASS" out of "U" and "ME".

❑ Problem-solving demands that we identify and question our unconscious assumptions. Indeed, we should be creative on assumptions – not close down by asking the question: '*What are all the assumptions we are making*' but open up by asking the group the question: '*What are all the possible assumptions we could be making?*'

❑ I demonstrate the power of this creative approach to assumptions by taking one of the creative thinking scenarios, used to practice GDT in the test phase. They used to be called "Lateral Thinking Questions."

❑ Originally, designers of these questions designed them thinking that there was only one right answer and trying to ensure that there was only one right answer.

❑ So the tutor would say to the groups. Here is a problem, "A man sold his dog and was killed on the way home". Now what is the answer to this problem? You will have to think "laterally" (or *"outside the box"* these days) in order to find it.

❑ So off the groups would go, or just work silently on their own in situ, and then one individual would shout out. *"Sir, Sir, I'm so very, very clever. I'm the bestest little creative thinker in the group. Ya! Boo! Sucks to You! – all you inferior people in my team or in this room. The answer is. "He was blind. He had sold his guide dog."*

❑ This did not do a power of good to the development of a high-performing team!

Application of the rule

❑ We now look at the creative thinking scenario: "a man sold his dog and was killed on the way home."

❑ As regards the answers, it is critically important that you use the 4th rule, "be creative on assumptions", to increase the range of answers.

❑ Now to a range of assumptions and answers:

- It could have been a very valuable dog, and the man was mugged for the money and died on the way home.

- It could have been a large, angry dog, which escaped from its new owners, and carried out a fatal revenge attack on his former master.

- It could have been a particular breed of dog, e.g. a husky. The man had sold the lead dog of his sled and had fallen into a crevasse and died.

- It could have been a guide dog, as his master was blind, and the blind man had been run over on the way home – the one right answer!

- It could have been his wife's dog whom she adored much, much more than hubbie and so she had shot her husband. (This is not strictly acceptable as the creative thinking scenario refers to "his" dog – but "No criticism rules OK". In any case, it is a general rule, made by the creative guru Edward de Bono, not to define a problem too closely, if you want to avoid missing out on potentially fantastic solutions. The problem would have been better put: "A man sold a dog and was killed on the way home," in which case there are many more solutions.)

- If you study the phrasing, there is nothing to stop you interpreting the sentence as to mean that the dog was killed on the way home – run over, eaten by the Chinese, killed by another dog and so on.

- You can argue that there is no connection between the two and then come up with as many answers as you like as to why a man should be killed on the way home!

TESTING

Now, what I say to the groups before they go off to practice GDT is:

Remember all the GDT rules

❑ If I have not promoted discovery of the rules, I always ensure the group(s) repeat them twice so that they have "sunk in". This is very important, as you want to minimise or eradicate any breaches, particularly of the no-criticism rule.

❑ This has become custom and habit to-left brained people and you don't want them to have to be told off for what is always an unintentional breach.

❑ Paradoxically, left-brained people love the word "rule" and once they have sunk in, they become great allies and drivers towards success, as they make sure all the rules are followed.

❑ They not only ensure that the no criticism rule is followed by all, but stop the right-brained people getting out of kilter – dashing ahead and coming up with their ideas on a creative thinking scenario that is not yet being considered by the group as a whole.

❑ I have printed up a number of scenarios that equals the total number in the largest group and suggested that they look at them all together sequentially. As mentioned, over enthusiastic individuals can get ahead of themselves and diminish the effectiveness of GDT.

Appoint rotating co-ordinators

❑ This is so that everyone gets a bite at the cherry and starts the process of enabling each team-member to develop coordinating skills, which, as you know, are critical to building an effective team.

❑ I suggest, when they get into their syndicate rooms, they agree the order of co-ordinators and, once that has been established, everyone reads the question, has a few moments to absorb the information, and then the co-ordinator manages the process and writes out all the ideas on the flipchart.

Have fun
❑ Humour is the engine of creativity

Come up with as many possible ideas as you can in the time available to explain each of the scenarios you are given.
❑ I allow 5 minutes per scenario and add on an extra 5, as people get totally absorbed in the exercise and time flies out of the window.

THE OUTCOMES PRODUCED

❑ When they have come back into plenary, if there is more than one group, then the set of answers for each question are provided on the basis of the particular co-ordinator leading the answers to the particular scenario with the other group's coordinators only adding additional solutions.

❑ I then rotate the lead co-ordinator so that total fairness is seen to prevail. There is an almost universal desire to be treated fairly, whatever the age or seniority of the individual.

Author's note:

My own view is that, unintentionally, a parent or parents preached fairness and practiced unfairness when the adults were children – see *Succeed as a Parent – ensure your children are your friends for life* as to why any such unfair treatment was unintentional and how to ensure there is no gap between words and actions with your children – if you have any, intend to have any or they are not already grown up.

❑ I must say that managing the feedback process is by far the most complicated matter for me, as I am having to multi-task, which is not a natural strength. I am delighted when I am dealing with only one group.

❑ I then ask three questions:

1. Does any individual in the room think that there would have been more ideas produced if you had gone away on your own to solve the problems?

The answer is a universal "no". So I point out that they have just experienced group creative synergy, i.e. The number of the ideas the group comes up with exceeds the sum of all the ideas, each individual would have come up, thinking on their own.

2. Was it just the one individual who came up with all the answers, or was it shared?

The universal answer is "shared".

3. So what does that prove?

Total silence usually follows this question. Whenever "promoting discovery" – my preferred approach – fails, I am more than happy to provide the "one right answer". My answer is: "It proves the point I made earlier that every individual can become more creative thanks to the power of GDT."

Author's note:

- As mentioned before, I have used the full recipe or the vital first two steps with over 1000 groups with staff varying from PAs and night-shift printers through managers, senior managers, and executives to CDMUs (Core Decision Making Units).
- These groups have been located in UK, US, Hong Kong, Thailand and Malaysia. With all the cultural diversity that exists in most countries, there has been a very wide range of "countries of origin" within a given country location for the programme.
- One client was located in 27 different countries. As the programmes were "global", we had an extraordinary range of different cultures represented.
- What was particularly enjoyable was "converting" one group of highly intellectual, left-brained, cynical and sceptical lawyers.
- There has been a 99.9% success rate in terms of achieving synergy and everyone agreeing to that outcome, with all the beneficial psychological impact that has, i.e. creating a belief in real team-working.

ENSURE YOU STAY TRUE TO YOUR OWN STYLE

❑ This is a continuing theme. I am not asking you to: "act out of character".

- You may be a "tell merchant", in which case tell them the rules, but remember to ensure the two times repetition (three times mentioned in all) so that the messages have "sunk in".
- You may be a "promoting discovery" merchant. In which case, "promote discovery".
- You may be somewhere in between, in which case cover GDT with a mixture.

❑ I can assure you that it works, whichever approach you adopt, though the "promoting discovery" approach takes longer.

❑ I favour the "promoting discovery" approach. However, on many development programmes for my clients, I have worked with one of my team of trainers that I recruited as my business expanded. I prefer to go solo, but many clients like to have diversity for their participants.

❑ I had one such trainer in my team, who was flexible by nature. This meant that he left everything to the last minute and did not show the same respect to time-tables, as a born organiser like my good self did.

❑ The GDT session, which I always ran, was the last session before lunch. In addition to the "attitude and actions" session, there was a house-keeping session, as well as time taken out to identify individual needs.

❑ So I lost a good half an hour on occasions and simply did a rather rapid "tell" session with no adverse effect on outcomes.

❑ My suggestion would be that you put the four rules on a prepared flip-chart, the questions in the Alaskan Electricity Example, and have a typed up hand-out of the creative thinking scenarios.

❑ You can cover the man and his dog scenario on the hoof or, if you have an artistic bent, draw a picture of a stick man and dog or even a little cartoon. First man with dog, then man without dog, then dead man.

❏ I used to do this very occasionally on the hoof (when I had the time) rather than pre-prepared. It acted as a sudden and pleasant difference in what had gone before and, as I cannot draw for toffee and my dog more often than not looked like a sheep, it generated some humour at my expense (I took it like a man). It was a good thing to do as humour is the engine of creativity and so it helped generate the right mood and ambience.

Author's note:

- I used the man and his dog as the example of "being creative on assumptions" when applying the recipe to the four comic actors on 31st January 2010.

- As I had written this section by then, I got rid of the "his" in front of the dog and it worked a treat. My drawing of the dog still has not improved with the passage of time! I used the comic strip approach.

❏ As to timings, I would set aside an hour and a quarter. Taking into account the half an hour for the "attitude and actions" session, the end of the GGT session marks the quarter of an hour coffee break.

CREATIVE THINKING SCENARIOS

1. A little girl, standing with her 2 parents by a river, looks at their reflection in the water, and says: "I can see all four of us". There are only three people present.

2. A woman, in despair, throws herself from the top of a skyscraper. It is a deliberate act of suicide. As she tumbles down, she hears a telephone ring, and cries out: "I wish I had not jumped".

3. A woman enters a field, and immediately dies. The pack on her back is empty.

4. A man stood looking through the window on the sixth floor of an office building. Suddenly, he was overcome by an impulse. He opened the window and leapt through it. He did not use a parachute or land on water or any special soft surface. Yet the man was completely unhurt when he landed.

5. Five men were proceeding down a country path. It began to rain. Four of the men quickened their step and began to walk faster. The fifth man made no effort to move any faster. However, he remained dry and the other four got wet. They all arrived at their destination together.

6. A policeman was called because a man was found lying unconscious outside a shop. As soon as the man came around, he was arrested. He was not a known criminal and had not been engaged in any kind of fight or dispute before losing consciousness.

7. A man and his golden retriever dog were found dead in the middle of a field. The man was wearing wading boots. No one else was around.

8. On a busy Friday afternoon, a man walked several miles across London from Westminster to Knightsbridge without being seen by anybody. The day was clear and bright. He did not travel by any method of transport other than by foot. London was thronged with people, yet not one of them saw him.

9. A man in a restaurant complained to the waiter that there was a fly in his cup of coffee. The waiter took the cup away and promised to bring a fresh cup of coffee. He returned a few moments later. The man tasted the coffee and complained that this was his original cup of coffee with the fly removed. He was correct.

10. A deserted yacht is found floating in the middle of the ocean and around it in the water are a dozen human corpses. There is no danger aboard the yacht and the yacht is not defective.

11. A farmer has two pigs. He sells them both on the same day at the same market, and each was sold for a fair price. Yet, when he sells them he gets 100 times more for one than the other.

12. A woman knocked on a stranger's door and asked to use the bathroom. She came out and killed the man with an axe.

13. A swimmer swam the 100 metre freestyle in a new world record. The pool, water and ambient conditions were all acceptable. The record was not allowed to stand.

14. Two frogs fell into a large cylindrical tank of cream and both fell to the bottom. The walls were sheer and slippery. One frog died but one survived.

15. A young girl was listening to the radio. Suddenly it went off for a minute, and then came back on again. There was nothing wrong with the radio or with the programme transmission from the radio station. She did not touch the radio controls.

16. A man is lying dead in a telephone booth. The telephone is off the hook, dangling down. Two of the windows are broken. He was not murdered.

17. A women lies awake unable to sleep. She makes a telephone call. 5 minutes later she is asleep.

18. A man watched his wife plunge head first down a deep ravine. He returned home to find her taking their dinner out of the microwave, completely unhurt.

19. A man is pushing a car, which stops next to a hotel. The man realises he is bankrupt.

20. An archaeological team discover two, very well preserved corpses, whilst excavating. The next day the newspapers proclaim: "Positive identification of Adam and Eve".

21. A naked man is found dead in a desert, clutching a straw. There are hills not far away and nothing but sand in the immediate vicinity.

Harness the Power of Process

INTRODUCTION

❑ This is the really meaty exercise, which takes up about half the time. It is where you use a very carefully designed process to progress your most important strategic issue into an action plan or plans which your team members will be enthusiastically committed to implement.

❑ What we will do is:

- Set out the complete process.
- Provide a real-life example of success.
- Analyse each step of the process.
- Consider the process whereby a team can achieve a given task in the most efficient and effective way.

❑ We then look at the final short session – the review.

SET OUT THE COMPLETE PROCESS

1. **Identify a single strategic issue that you/your group is interested in developing**

   e.g. We will improve our work/life balance.

2. **Develop statement of intent with time-frame**

   e.g. In two years, we will have achieved an effective work/life balance.

3. Determine what success looks like

What will it look/feel like operating with an effective work/life balance? What will be happening that will guarantee that we have an effective work/life balance?

4. Determine how to measure success

What quantifiable measure or measures should be introduced so that we know that we have achieved an effective work/life balance?

5. Determine what needs to be done to achieve success

Use GDT to come up with as many ideas/suggestions as possible that will create an effective work/life balance.

6. Agree the top 4 priorities for implementation

- Each individual in the group determines the 4 priorities they would personally select for implementation, allocating 4 points to their first choice, 3 to their second, 2 to their third and 1 to their last choice.

- When every individual has made their decision, each comes to the flip-chart and puts the number against the ideas selected.

- The top 4 ideas have the highest aggregate totals.

7. Develop the process plan in each priority area

For each priority area, determine:

- What should be done first and why?
- What should be done second and why? and so on.
- Then complete each plan by putting approximate timings for the sequence of activities.

Author's note:

❏ I have taken this from the brief on the process in a work-book. Of course, you would not need an hour and three quarters to solve this particular issue. Roughly 10 seconds.

❏ The answer is: "ensure that every employee in our organisation is working in an effective team in 3 months by implementing Project Omega for Organisations, set out in Appendix 1."

PROVIDE AN EXAMPLE OF SUCCESS

❏ A number of my clients asked me to apply this process model with groups of their managers on a given programme. The managers would be provided with the key strategic issues the company had identified as part of their overall game plan.

❏ They would then select an issue and progress it through to an action plan, which would be typed up and sent to the CEO – a very neat way of getting effective input into strategy development.

❏ I have had a number of City Law firms in the past as clients and this is the presentation made by one of the groups of associate lawyers who completed the process. The programme was run in 2002.

EXAMPLE

1. Identify a single strategic issue that your group is interested in developing.

• Retaining high quality associates.

2. Develop statement of intent with time-frame.

• By May 2004, new system in place.
• By May 2006, results outlined in (3) below obtained.

---

3. Determine what success looks like.

- Deliver higher quality of work to clients.
- Increase in profitability.
- Higher morale among associates at all levels.
- Retain more high quality senior associates.

4. Determine how to measure success.

- Improved retention rate among identified high value associates.
- Has profitability increased?
- Has morale improved (associate/partner survey)?
- Have we delivered high quality work?
- Client buy in.

5. How to achieve success:

- Establish distinct career path for senior associates that is an alternative to (but neither a bar nor a necessary precursor to) partnership.
- Implement genuinely flexible remuneration and reward package for senior associates (currently there appears to be little or no flexibility in practice).
- Have transparent policy on senior associate career path.

6. Process plan:

a. Distinct career path

- Consultation among partners, associates and clients.
- Research into how our and other firms have made use of counsel positions – lessons learned.
- Determine nature of role and policy to implement.
- Pilot/test in different offices.
- Global implementation May 2006.

b. Flexible remuneration

- Research packages at other law firms (inc. US) and other employers.
- Seek feedback from senior associates.
- Determine what can be flexible in terms of pay and other benefits.
- Committee of partners, HR and senior associates draft transparent policy.
- Finalise policy.
- Follow policy in practice through consultation with senior associates.

c. Policy on career path

- Consultation with senior associates.
- Committee of partners, HR and senior associates draft policy.
- Finalise policy and publish on intranet.
- Annual meetings (separate from appraisals) among each senior associate, a partner (not necessarily line manager) and an HR representative to assess progress by reference to the policy.

Author's note:

❑ You will note that step 7 has become step 6 as the voting for priorities has not been recorded. Rightly, senior executives are not interested in how their managers decided on the priorities, only on the results. So we never typed this up.

❑ However, I provide an example of the voting system in action for a decision-making unit in the next section.

ANALYSE EACH STEP OF THE PROCESS

1. IDENTIFY A SINGLE STRATEGIC ISSUE THAT YOU/YOUR GROUP IS INTERESTED IN DEVELOPING

Two questions arise:

- ❑ Why a single issue?
- ❑ How to decide which issue?

Why a single issue?

❑ I have noticed that, if two people focus in their discussion on a single issue, they, typically, get their act together, progress the problem and finish the conversation on a high with a commitment to meet up again. If there are multiple issues, then one or other gets distracted and the conversation and the relationship lose its way.

❑ The other reason to use a single issue is thanks to Sir Brian Pitman, who was appointed CEO of the then Lloyds Bank in 1983. It was the worst performing bank amongst the then big four clearers – Lloyds, Barclays, Midland and NatWest. In the period 1983 – 1989, he increased profits by an annual average of 30% and Lloyds Bank became the best performing (i.e. most profitable) clearer. His quote to me was: "Effective strategy requires focus and hard choices."

❑ The need for a single issue is not generally recognised. This the issue that the particular group selected to consider:

"Recruiting, training, developing and retaining the brightest and best-motivated graduates to maintain the quality of the firm"

❑ When I pointed out the importance of focusing on a single issue, they chose the one, naturally, in which they had most personal interest.

How to decide which issue?

❑ I would imagine that this will spring out, as everyone will know *and* it will be your most important issue. What many leaders fail to realise is that not only do "great minds think alike" but so too do a collection of great minds, i.e. team minds think alike.

❑ Brian Edwards, who kindly provided a quote for this book, when he had experienced the St Ives development programme, came up with the excellent quote: "*An effective leader or coach provides motivation on a voyage of discovery, where common sense prevails*". Effective group working enables the discovery of that common sense.

❑ Two case studies illustrate this key point:

ASK THE RIGHT QUESTION

A large insurance company recognised that, to survive and grow in rapidly changing market conditions, it would have to change its customer base and distribution channels – two very significant changes.

So the Board spent 6 months developing its strategy in considerable detail. They were poised to roll out the strategy, when a junior board member asked the right question. "We know that we have developed the best strategy, but how are we going to motivate our senior managers to implement it?"

Their response was remarkable and remarkably effective. They flew all their senior managers to Copenhagen for 3 days, split them up into teams, and presented them with the problems and all the research findings – but none of the Board's strategy.

There were two outcomes:

1. They came up with the same strategic response.

2. They were fully motivated to implement it, which they did. This included some of those managers making themselves redundant!

LEADING FROM BEHIND

I and a colleague ran a three day strategy development and team-building programme for the then DERA (Defence and Research Agency). The programme was run for Sir John Chisholm, the CEO, and the top 32 decision-takers in the various businesses.

What was very interesting about this programme was that Sir John had developed a very clear view beforehand of the vision, strategic direction and key actions required. At the end of the programme, all the teams had developed exactly the same view – but they had discovered it for themselves and so were committed to it.

It is an example of effective leadership, as defined by Dwight Eisenhower: "Leadership is the art of getting someone else to do something you want done because they want to do it". Sir John Chisholm is now Chairman of the Medical Research Council.

However, if there is a lack of clarity amongst the group, then you can use the process set out under step 6, which we will come to shortly.

2. DEVELOP STATEMENT OF INTENT WITH TIME-FRAME

❏ The phrase "statement of intent" has been used deliberately. Typically, Western companies use left-brained words like goals, objectives and targets, which result in hard measures and too narrow a focus, all of which does nothing to motivate the employee.

❏ You may be aware that the Japanese grew from small local players to global giants. The first thing they did was to form a "statement of strategic intent", e.g. Komatsu's "statement of strategic intent" was to "encircle Caterpillar", and it was successful.

❑ These could be 20 years out, but were used to focus all the employees on a single motivational goal ("beat the competition").

❑ They then set a series of "Corporate Challenges" – what we in the West refer to as interim milestones. Employees are much more motivated to "rise to a challenge" than aim for a milestone.

❑ A corporate challenge was set, typically, for a three year period, one all the employees could easily relate too – not too far away on the horizon. The first corporate challenge selected was the one that would be most effective in achieving the "strategic intent". It was, for all the Japanese companies, to provide total quality.

❑ Now, interestingly, the Japanese operated a system called Keretsu. This was nationwide and meant that all companies in a given industry (and across industries) shared knowledge and the development of the appropriate technology to make the given dream come true.

❑ With our excessively competitive industries, very little of that was going on (no critical mass of investment developing) and, of course, there was no united front or focus within a given company.

❑ Hence the successful "zero defects" policy and the "just-in-time" delivery systems and the eradication of our indigenous motor car manufacturing industry to name but one.

3. DETERMINE WHAT SUCCESS LOOKS LIKE

This is whole-brained, combining a mission and a vision. If you look back to the lawyers' answers we have:

Mission
❑ Increase in profitability

Vision
❑ Deliver higher quality of work to clients
❑ Higher morale among associates at all levels
❑ Retain more high quality senior associates

Author's note:
Left-brained lawyers use "dry", "matter of fact" language to describe a right-brained vision. If they had all been Martin Luther Kings, then it would have been along the lines of: *"We have a dream, where only people who are motivated, enthusiastic and caring work for us, where our clients love us, because we love them and delight them all the time."* (*"And where we make a small fortune as a result"* – to integrate the vision with the mission.)

4. DETERMINE HOW TO MEASURE SUCCESS
This combines quantitative measures for the left-brained "mission" and qualitative measures for the right-brained "vision".

5. DETERMINE WHAT NEEDS TO BE DONE TO ACHIEVE SUCCESS

❑ You will find that, as you have applied GDT in the recent past, the creative momentum will be carried forward, providing, of course, the behavioural and process rules are being religiously followed.

❑ You will come up with quite a few ideas quickly and it may only take a few minutes. There is no need to prolong it, after you have run out of steam.

❑ I will take another real-life example from an in-tact team with 7 team-members and 3 status divisions. The strategic issue selected was, "beating the competition". I cannot recall what industry they were in, but just set out the ideas below.

1. Take them over
2. Better information
3. Improve skills
4. Better service to customers
5. Be cheaper
6. Innovate
7. Noble them
8. Cheat
9. Better advertising budget
10. One stop shop
11. Better added value
12. Use of technology
13. Let them take us over

6. AGREE THE TOP 4 PRIORITIES FOR IMPLEMENTATION

❏ Each individual in the group determines the 4 priorities they would personally select for implementation, allocating 4 points to their first choice, 3 to their second, 2 to their third and 1 to their last choice.

❏ When every individual has made their decision, each comes to the flip-chart and puts the number against the ideas selected.

❏ The top 4 ideas have the highest aggregate totals.

Key points

❏ This process was the only thing of value that I gained from a day and a half's attendance at some work-shop on some "unique" approach to creative thinking given by an individual whose name I cannot recall. It was during 1996 to 1997. I have quite a good memory, but it is, as all are, selective.

❏ Its value is that it accords with the principles of effective team-working, i.e. sharing decision-taking rather than the traditional approach of the leader making the decisions.

The example

❑ The seven man team applied step six to produce the following, with the individual rankings and total scores at the end of each idea.

1. Take them over
2. Better information (see note at end)}
3. Improve skills (2,2,2,1,1,3 = 9)
4. Better service to customers (4,4,4,3,2,3 = 20)
5. Be cheaper
6. Innovate (3,3,2,4,4,2 = 18)
7. Noble them
8. Cheat
9. Better advertising budget (1)
10. One stop shop (3)
11. Better added value (2,4,4 = 10)
12. Use of technology (1,1,3,2,1 = 8)
13. Let them take us over

Note
• During the marking process, one team-member pointed out that they could use technology to get information on competitors and all agreed the information marks could be subsumed into the technology idea.

❑ We now summarise the top ideas, with total marks allocated in brackets.

• Better service to customers (20)
• Innovate (18)
• Better added value (10)
• Improve skills (9)
• Use of technology (8)

❑ It is interesting to note that the top five ideas represented 93% of the marks allocated – confirming the point about achieving consensus.

❑ This particular group, having studied the results , decided that the team as a whole would focus on driving through better service to customers (the starting point being asking customers to determine current performance in all the service elements, and which were most important to them) with individuals/sub-groups, who had the sub-issue as a personal choice, focusing on developing them.

❑ At that time, I had not developed the full 7-step process model (it was only 4) and so they did not carry out the final step 7.

7. DEVELOP THE PROCESS PLAN IN EACH PRIORITY AREA

❑ For each priority area, determine:

- What should be done first and why?
- What should be done second and why? And so on.
- Then complete each plan by putting approximate timings for the sequence of activities.

❑ I worked out this questioning approach to developing a process plan in 1996, when I was part of a "team" simulating "meeting a client's needs". The first team-member had identified the needs and I was the team-member who was asked to lead the development of a plan to meet those needs.

❑ The "team" was a group of competitors for a position in a small high-powered HR consultancy firm. We were being assessed in a "real-life" situation by our putative new employer.

❑ I got the job, resigned from the management centre, but changed my mind when I discovered, through my mole, that the HR Director had started an affair with the Managing Director.

❑ Fortunately, I was "enticed" back into the fold with a pay rise of over 20% of basic salary. I had stayed loyal and committed to my existing employer and was the most utilised consultant at the time.

❑ There were over 600 applicants for the single job. Chapter 10 of *Succeed at Work – take the fast track to the top is entitled*, "Get any job you go for."

❑ Incidentally the key components of my book *Ask the Right Question – tips and techniques to transform your key relationships* (published in the UK in 1997, USA in 1998 and Japan in 2003) form part of chapter 3 of the *Succeed at Work* book. The title of that chapter is, "Become a Brilliant Communicator (Part 1)"

❑ Finally, on the advertising front, I left Sundridge Park Management Centre in October 2008 to set up my own training and development business. I ran the business for 6 and half years. During that period, the annual average equivalent of my take-home pay was just over three times my actual take-home pay in my last year of employment. Chapter 11 of *Succeed at Work* is entitled, "Run a Successful Business".

TIMINGS

❑ One and three quarter hours is given for this session. As with the GDT session, groups get totally absorbed in this exercise – especially as it is dealing with the real thing – resolving an important strategic issue, which, if done well , which it will be, means you have all taken a giant step forward in terms of increasing both efficiency and effectiveness of output.

❑ It may be that you can complete action plans (a process plan is simply determining the right actions in the right time order) for all the top four or five priority areas. Maybe only one.

❑ The minimum goal is to achieve a process plan for the number one priority, before calling a halt at 12.45. I have never come across a group that has not achieved that – but either take on yourself or allocate the role to a group member of "watching the clock", having agreed approximate timings for each of the seven steps.

❑ If you actually complete process plans in all the priority areas, then call a halt, start the review and you can have an early lunch.

THE PROCESS TO COMPLETE A TEAM TASK

❑ Our outdoor development guru David Butler produced a very effective 10 step process, i.e. sequence of activities to achieve a team task.

❑ This was considered so effective by Brian Edwards, the CEO of St Ives plc, that he arranged for small, laminated pocket cards to be produced and distributed to all the managers attending their development programmes. On the front of each card was the 10 step process to complete a team task and on the reverse was the process required to give praise effectively and to give constructive criticism effectively, (see *Succeed as a Leader – become the boss from heaven not hell*).

❑ The "task" is any brief that you have received internally (from on high) or externally (from a client) and the intention is that you work together as a team.

❑ We set out the ten steps, and then amplify each step:

1. Appoint a co-ordinator.
2. Clarify the brief.
3. Ensure everyone understands the brief.
4. Check your resources.
5. Initiate the Group Discovery Technique.
6. Select at least two ideas.
7. Develop and plan your first choice.
8. Test it out.
9. Review
10. Implement

1. APPOINT A CO-ORDINATOR

❑ That will come as no surprise. You should be the first co-ordinator for your work-shop. However, as already mentioned, once the group has developed maturity, you should rotate the position to ensure that, over time, everyone has the opportunity to co-ordinate (or be the process facilitator).

❑ Ask for volunteers, as the team-members who are the most confident (usually the extroverts) will be at the head of the queue. When it gets to Buggins turn (Buggins being the least confident and usually an introvert), he or she will have observed many examples of success and will know how to succeed themselves.

2. CLARIFY THE BRIEF

❑ This is the time to uncover those implicit, invalid assumptions. With projects, as we now know, it is usually insufficient challenge and exploration at the start that leads to confusion and poor execution. Often, in this phase, you can produce a smarter objective or find a neat way to complete the project.

❑ The classic example of this was the first outdoor exercise where the teams were blindfolded. So we will take time out to consider two case studies, one where the team is thrown in the deep end with no knowledge about effective team-working or the need for co-ordination and the other where the team has appointed the coordinator, is fully aware of the process and has gone through the first two steps of the recipe.

THROWN IN THE DEEP END

Imagine that you and five of your colleagues from work have been magically transported to the middle of a grassy glade in a sunlit wood in the height of summer. You have all agreed to complete some tasks, which will help you learn how to be more effective as a team.

You have completed a few warm-up exercises to get used to the new environment and are being introduced to the first task, which you and your colleagues have to complete in 30 minutes.

You have been asked to put on blindfolds, and are still recovering from the shock of having to work in the dark, literally, when the instructor throws some equipment into the middle of the group of six, and utters the statement: "With the equipment provided, form a perfect square and place yourselves equidistant around the outside of it."

Can you guess how you would be all feeling, and what happens next?

As you will appreciate, there is a lot of uncertainty and discomfort. When operating in such an environment, we want answers. We want to remove the uncertainty and gain a little bit of security, as quickly as we can.

The individuals in the group rush to find out what the equipment actually is, with a few near misses, when it comes to the bumping of heads. The equipment is a very long piece of rope; say 20 metres, neatly curled up.

The pattern of behaviour and actions taken are as follows:

- To begin with, and for some considerable time, there is maximum heat and minimum light. Some group members talk at each other – vying for the leadership. Helpful suggestions by other group members like: "Shall we nominate one person to co-ordinate our efforts" or: "Let's not implement one idea, before we have explored all the options" are completely lost in the noise.

- The individual who can get the group to listen to his or her idea first (shouting the loudest) becomes the leader – but leadership follows the development of the idea, changing when some-one else modifies the idea or takes over implementation.

93

- There comes a time when the majority are locked into one solution, and any alternative put forward is dismissed out of hand.

- Clarity of communication is poor because of the over-reliance on words (although the amount of unseen gesticulation is very high!). Towards the end, people are doing what they are told to do by the task leader, quite cheerfully but badly, with little understanding of what they are actually doing and why.

- In the middle phase, there is sub-grouping with no cross-communication. Additionally, there are one or two individuals completely turned off, just standing holding the rope, waiting morosely for something to happen.

- Once everyone has got hold of a bit of the rope, there is considerable reluctance to let it go – holding on for dear life. Indeed, in many groups, only solutions which permit continuous holding of the rope by all members are implemented.

- In most groups, the standard solution involves full use of the rope with an attempt to produce an enormous square.

- Individuals can become quite dogmatic, not only locking into the "one right answer" but also into a completely wrong answer. For instance, one individual in one group asserted strongly that there were two ropes. This was accepted by the group as a whole and a solution developed and implemented until the evidence against the proposition became overwhelming.

- Most solutions involve activity by all towards the end. Then, individuals begin to believe that they will succeed, energy levels and commitment soar, and the end comes much more quickly than external observers anticipate. It is as if 90% of the time is spent in confusion and muddle, and, almost magically, a result is achieved right at the end. In this case, it is: "Necessity is the mother of action."

- Some groups never make it, but those that do, before they take off their blindfolds, are very satisfied with the outcome. For most groups, that satisfaction is severely diminished when they see a very imperfect square or there has been no attempt to place themselves "equidistant around it", as everyone forgot that part of the brief or, they forgot the word "outside" and are all inside the rope.

Although lack of sight exaggerates our behaviours, managers recognise that what happens in this exercise is a fair reflection of behaviours and actions that unformed teams or immature groups exhibit at work, which is, as we have mentioned in the introduction, the norm in the work-place.

SMALL IS BEAUTIFUL

Now imagine that you are well on the way to becoming an effective team, having covered attitudes and actions and GDT and you have all learnt, to a lesser or greater extent, the process model – being blindfolded tends to unfocus the mind.

You have been appointed the co-ordinator, and we will call you RTB (Rapid Team Builder). Your team-members are George, Alice, Mark, Zainol and Lucia. The starting point is the same. You have all received the instruction: "With the equipment provided, form a perfect square and place yourselves equidistant around the outside of it".

RTB (With considerable authority): "Now team, before we do anything, let us make sure we all understand the brief. Alice, can you remember what the instructor just said?"

Alice: "Well, er, I think he said that: 'With the equipment provided, form a perfect square.'"

RTB: "Thanks, Alice – was that all?"

Zainol: "No, I don't think so. Didn't he also say that, when we have formed a perfect square with the equipment provided, we should place ourselves equidistant around the outside of it?"

RTB: "Well done, Zainol. You're right."

RTB continues: "George, would you mind summarising for us, so that we all know exactly what we have to achieve."

George: "With the equipment provided, we have to form a perfect square, and then place ourselves equidistant around the outside of it."

RTB: "Excellent. Now we all know what we have to do. We need to find out what this "equipment provided" is precisely. Lucia and Zainol, could you kneel down, investigate and when you both agree, tell us what you find?"

A minute goes by.

Lucia: "It's a long piece of rope – just a single rope and it is difficult to measure precisely – but it must be around 20 metres, as it is 20 of Zainol's arm lengths."

RTB: "Thank you, Lucia and Zainol, We know what we have to do, and we now know what the equipment is. Let us put our thinking hats on and question the brief – in case we are making unnecessary assumptions, which will reduce the quality of the solution. "Form a perfect square with the long rope provided and place ourselves equidistant around the outside of the rope." Any questions on the brief?"

Pause

Mark: "I have had a thought – do we need to use all the rope to form the square – couldn't we just use a small portion of the rope and then place ourselves around that – much easier than trying to form a very large square."

RTB: "That's an interesting idea. It doesn't say "using all the equipment", just "using the equipment" in the brief. What do the others think?"

General agreement ensues.

I will not continue the conversation through to the end, as we have seen enough to realise how an RTB performs. However, they did, with this questioning approach, realise that "equidistant around the outside of it" had been deliberately vaguely worded to allow a number of interpretations.

Typically, immature groups read it as meaning that they had to place themselves at an equal distance from each other around the square, which was a veritable nightmare when you had 5 to 7 – especially with a rope that is 20 metres long.

[David Butler showed no mercy. If the group size was 4, then they had to form an equilateral triangle!]

This group (and a few other groups) recognised that they could all be equidistant from the centre of the square, but standing outside the rope. This was extremely easy to achieve, when you had a very small square.

Indeed they achieved both types of equidistance. (I keep referring to this group, as it was the only group that was successful, whose actual conversation I wrote down.)

Within 10 minutes, blindfolds were removed to display a team of six people, with arms linked (not hands with variable length of arms) around a neat little square of rope.

You should have heard the cry of triumph that went up, when they saw the result, which they instinctively knew they had achieved before sight was restored.

Author's note:

❑ Life, they say, is a continuous learning experience. I have just discovered something in writing up this case study. The third step, which we come to next, is: "Ensure everyone understands the brief."

❑ However, quite rightly, RTB gained understanding of the brief, and then checked the equipment, before "clarifying the brief". In real life, you are never going to have a piece of rope as critical equipment, essential to completing the brief – but perhaps the order should be 1, 3,2,4 – changing the mindset of a decade!!!

❑ As mentioned, I had discovered the questioning approach to determining the right process (step 7) in 1996. We had been using David's process model for years and so it had become "habit and custom". I never thought to apply the questioning approach to this "tried and tested" model. If I had, it would have produced the right order.

❑ It is also interesting to note how you can steer a group, when "promoting discovery" of the model or any "truth" for that matter. One individual might say that step two should be "understand the brief" and we would suggest that it should be "clarify the brief" and that would be accepted.

❑ It is not that vital, because, as long as both occur, that is the main thing and the rest of the model is very robust. Still it is an eye-opener as to the damaging power of mindset or: *"This is the way we have always done it – so this is the right way to do it."*

3. ENSURE EVERYONE UNDERSTANDS THE BRIEF

❑ It is vital that everyone: "sings from the same hymn sheet," i.e. is clear about and fully understands the brief/objective/task as refined. Remember to ask an open question, e.g. "Sheila, do you mind recapping to make sure we are all clear" (which is long-form for: "What is the brief?") or recap yourself. Avoid the closed question: "Do we all understand the brief". You will get the answer, "Yes", as people do not want to admit ignorance in front of their peers or their boss.

❑ Indeed, before moving to the next step, it is worth asking your group as a final check: "Any final questions before we move on as it is critically important that we have the same understanding of the brief" – then pause.

Author's note:

This is, of course, what RTB did.

4. CHECK YOUR RESOURCES

❑ Develop a provisional time plan for the rest of the planning phases, as well as implementation.

❑ Identify which individuals have what skills to complete the task to a high standard. Having an amateur sailor is very helpful in this exercise.

❑ What occasionally happens is that one team member has done the exercise before in a different life. That is more often than not a complete disaster as that individual becomes the task leader, the process goes out of the window (unless you have a very strong co-ordinator) and there can be a strain on the team dynamics, when they find out that other teams have done it faster and with a neater solution.

❑ Identify any additional resource requirements over and above what is currently available.

Author's note:

❑ This is why, in real life, step 4 stays where it is. You want to make sure that the resources are driven by a complete understanding of the task, the achievement of which may have changed the resource requirement as the result of uncovering invalid implicit assumptions.

5. INITIATE THE GROUP DISCOVERY TECHNIQUE (GDT)

❑ As RTB, you make sure that the rules are followed – particularly the no criticism rule. This includes self-criticism.

- The number of times (when the groups are doing the next set of tasks without blindfolds) I have seen the co-ordinator get too involved with coming up with ideas himself – lost control of the process – is legion.

- The number of times I have seen individuals wander off, sometimes even the co-ordinator, to play around with the equipment is legion.

- The number of times that the wanderer has picked up a piece of equipment and come up with a really neat solution is legion.

- The number of times that individual has dropped the piece or pieces of equipment and, before wandering back to the group, shaken her or his head and muttered, "it won't work", is, most unfortunately, also legion.

❑ You will notice that RTB stayed focussed on the process and asked the open probing questions and did not come up with the change to the brief.

❑ Your primary role is to ensure that the process is followed in the right order and everyone follows the process. You can also come up with brilliant ideas yourself – but that should always be secondary.

❑ You may have noticed that RTB was quite authoritative, when required. A good RTB is a good controller of people. They never take offence, as said before, as they have all agreed both to the behavioural rules and the process rules.

6. SELECT AT LEAST TWO IDEAS

The favourite to enable the development of plan A and the reserve to enable the development of plan B, if plan A doesn't work out in practice.

7. DEVELOP AND PLAN YOUR FIRST CHOICE

Who does what, why, where and when? This is the time to allocate roles. A new role is the task manager – the individual who is best suited to manage the implementation of the plan. It could be the coordinator, who has been looking out for the team – managing the process to date – or a different individual. Whoever it is, there still needs to be a coordinator, taking the "bird's eye" view. This ensures that:

❑ The group dynamics are not damaged by the task manager focusing on the task and not the people. (Harriet's blubbing in the corner.)

❑ There is not too much divergence from the plan in the next phase.

8. TEST IT OUT

See if plan A works out in practice. If it does, excellent. If it does not, then you fall back on plan B. Depending on resource requirements for the original idea, time can be saved if both ideas are being developed, planned and tested in parallel by sub-groups.

9. REVIEW

You do this to ensure that everyone in the group fully understands who is doing what, when and why.

10. IMPLEMENT

Key Point

Invariably, any team that follows this process will complete the task ahead of schedule to an extremely high standard. This is why Brian Edwards ensured the laminated cards were produced and distributed to all his managers.

THE REVIEW

❑ Returning to the recipe, at 12.45, you move into the final short step – the review of the experience.

❑ To ensure you finish on a high, you only accentuate the positive. Specifically, you ask the team two questions.

    1. What are all the things we have done well as a team to produce this excellent performance?

    2. What should we do to perform even better as a team?

❑ This way, you ensure you: "start with a bang and finish with a firework display."

6

Recipe for Action

Exercise	Outcomes	On flip-chart	Hand-outs	Time
"Attitude & Actions"	* Discovery and commitment to the behaviours of a high-performing team. * Agreement that all team-members ensure they are followed.	Key words, e.g. *Attitudes & Actions *Any high-performing team *Sharing from experience	None	09.00 to 09.30
GDT	*Consensus on the achievement of creative group synergy. *Consensus that the individual becomes more creative by participating in GDT.	*The four rules *The Alaskan Electricity Company Questions *A dog and a man?	Creative Thinking Scenarios	09.30 to 10.45

Exercise	Outcomes	On flip-chart	Hand-outs	Time
Break	N/A	N/A	N/A	10.45 to 11.00
Strategic Planning Process	Commitment to implement the strategic action plan or plans produced	None	The 7 step template **and** example of successful use	11.00 to 12.45
Team review	Commitment by all to actions to ensure the team goes from "strength to strength"	Key questions 1. What are all the things we have done well as a team to produce this excellent performance? 2. What should we do to perform even better as a team?	None	12.45 to 13.00

7

Break Free from "Received Wisdom"

INTRODUCTION

❑ I am making some key points at this stage, because you have now discovered the recipe.

❑ What this chapter looks at first is how "received wisdom" has denied the ability to build effective teams both outside and in the work-place, as well as making it impossible to achieve any form of down streaming. Specifically we look at the following:

- Expert's scientific approach
- Progression to performance
- External team-builder
- I must be there
- Throw in the deep end
- Recipe unknown

Author's note:
The first two are re-enforcement of messages covered in the introduction. I will plead the need for repetition to harness the power of SPO (**S**ubconscious **P**sychological **O**smosis) in justification.

❑ We then turn to what I refer to as the 6 "C"s, i.e. levels, stages, phases and lock-ins. I will explain the difference in the main body of the text. Barry Tuckman developed the fairly widely known "forming", "storming", "norming" and "performing" stages. Specifically, we look at:

- "Confusion" or "Forming"
- "Conflict" or "Storming"
- "Control" lock-ins
- "Cooperative" or "Norming"
- "Consensus" lock-in
- "Commitment" or "Performing"

❑ With each of these "stages", we consider where these different stages or phases fit into the idea of development levels. Teams, like individuals, go from an immature or undeveloped state with low confidence, self esteem and poor performance to a mature or highly developed state with a high confidence and high performance.

EXPERT'S SCIENTIFIC APPROACH

❑ All the experts, whether Meredith Belbin or Margerison and McCann or Bale, took a scientific approach to the study of groups or teams. This meant that they formed experimental groups, and simply observed them in action – left them to their own devices.

❑ Interference was verboten, as that would break the independence and therefore validity of any results. So the focus was on the individual operating in the team and not the team itself.

❑ Therefore, and it took an age, (and we will continue using Belbin as the exemplar, as he is most widely known), when eventually a high-performing team emerged, the key "research finding" was the fact that all the team-roles were present without excessive duplication, avoiding "personality clashes".

❑ There was a little ray of sunshine in that that one of the necessary functions was co-ordinating – but personalised so that you focussed on the individual, who had a preference to be a co-ordinator.

❑ The fact that the co-ordinator needed to be the team-leader or, if the team-leader was strong in other areas, he or she needed to develop co-ordinating skills (as you have done) was missed.

❑ Much more importantly, the focus on the individual in the team and the inevitable personalisation of team-roles rather than recognising the team needed to carry out varies functions in a well-defined, clearly understood process meant that building an effective team at all, never mind rapidly, was a very remote possibility.

❑ It also leads to the next piece of, "received wisdom".

PROGRESSION TO PERFORMANCE

❑ If there no recognition of and hence guidance in how to build an effective team, then any group, if left to its own devices, will go into a "conflict" or "storming" stage. They may stay there and end up in the extreme case, when having crash-landed in South America, eating each other.

❑ However, if the mix/leadership is such that there is some progression, they will move on to the "co-operative" or "forming" stage.

❑ Now they may move into a lock-in stage "consensus" (which is covered later) but some will eventually get to the "commitment" level or "performing" stage.

❑ So the mindset was formed and is now universal that, to create a high-performing team, it has to progress through these four stages. As you have discovered, this is not true. But again, this made building an effective team at all, never mind rapidly, a very remote possibility – particularly because of the belief that you had to have, "blood on the carpet."

Author's note:
The combination of these two inappropriate mindsets leads to completely the wrong approach to team-building in organisations, as exemplified by the case study, "I say no to profitable business".

I SAY NO TO PROFITABLE BUSINESS

Many years ago, I was invited to tender for some highly profitable business, which was to build an effective team from an executive group of five individuals. Being executives, they expected to pay very high daily and preparation rates, as otherwise they would not be getting the quality they deserved.

Unfortunately, I was not interviewed by a member of the team but by a high-powered consultant, who was advising them. She explained that the key reason for current poor performance was a personality clash between two team-members, i.e. they hated each other's guts.

It was the CEO and the Marketing Director, both strong shapers. The CEO had been promoted from Marketing Director and a new Marketing Director had been hired in 6 months earlier. The CEO was making that individual's life an absolute misery, as he interfered in all the bits that he had enjoyed doing, before being promoted to the top job. It is very lonely, if you "don't do teams", at the top. He would have been very isolated and so, psychologically speaking, needed to return to his comfort zone.

She suggested that the best way of proceeding was that the two rutting stags both filled in the appropriate psychometrics and then, armed with the results, I should have confidential one-on-one discussions with them, so that I could see both sides of the picture and pour some oil on troubled waters.

She added that it would be a good idea (so that these two would not appear to have been picked on) if I did exactly the same with the other three team members, but the focus of my discussions with them should be on getting their take on this critical problem.

Quite clearly, money was no object and, from her point of view, she was doing a damage limitation exercise, so that the inevitable "conflict" that took place when I started to build the team would be minimised.

She did not, of course, believe that a team could be built bypassing the conflict stage and that, once this had been achieved, their differences would have been marginalised and more importantly, the feedback session (see chapter 9) would mean that all the team members would "own up" to the key problems in key relationships that had occurred, as well producing action plans to both maintain the momentum of the team and resolve any residual relationship problems.

Needless to say, I did not tender for the business, and I doubt very much that those executives ever worked as an effective unit.

EXTERNAL TEAM-BUILDER

❑ This is inevitable. A team in trouble calls in outside help to sort out their difficulties. Readers of this book will be the first team-leaders in situ in the world to be able build their own teams into a high-performing unit (in, of course, only 4 hours).

❑ Hence organisations will be able to collect together a group of RTBs and complete Project Omega for Organisations, which enables nearly every employee to be working in an effective team within 3 months of commencement – see Appendix 1.

❑ Even if the external facilitator has succeeded in building an effective team, then there can be no down streaming or up streaming, because the team goes back to perform better in their work roles, which is why the facilitator was called in, in the first place, and not to, "spread the gospel".

❏ Even if some individual in the team decided that they wanted to change roles, (highly unlikely), then they have not got the gospel as they were being done to rather than doing the doing.

I MUST BE THERE

❏ All facilitators I have come across are hard-wired to be with the group at all times. Their clients expect them to be there all the time, as do the delegates. They are paid to be there.

❏ Now I am hardly ever there. All the testing is done by the groups operating on their own. I am there for the input and discussion and for the feedback and review of outcomes. Early on, I used to pop in all the time and say: "any problems, any questions".

❏ When I was still in this phase, I used to get great delight when I heard the response, "bog off, we can don't need your help" – put slightly more politely. It helped me take the decision to stay clear.

❏ I had, quite happily, stayed clear, when a technical skills trainer. The difference was that then all the delegates were junior to me and my boss had complete faith in me, whereas now it was a cultural norm and the delegates were all paying punters.

❏ The critical point is that, if a facilitator is always there, he or she will feel the need to intervene or make some wise comment or helpful suggestion to justify their presence. Equally one or more team-members will call upon this resource.

❏ This means that the group can never become a self-managing unit/high-performing team.

❏ Often, where the facilitator is particularly good and wise, a dependency culture is created, which is great for the facilitator's ego but again denies the ability to ever achieve the desired outcome – building an effective team.

THROW IN THE DEEP END

❑ This is universal practice, both in the work-place and on development programmes. It is so incredibly stupid. What is the point of throwing some-one, who cannot swim, into a swimming pool and watch her or him drown, when, with a little bit of coaching and support, she or he could have become an Olympic Gold Medallist?

❑ Again it is another strongly held-mindset combining two aspects.
  1. "I was thrown in at the deep end and I swam (eventually, after nearly drowning a couple of times). So should every-body else."
  2. "I have always been a great believer in the excellent Roman practice of leaving new-born male babies out in the cold on a winter's night – without any clothes on. Some died and some survived. The ones that survived were going to be proper real men. The ones who died would have been wimps. We only want real men in our work-place."

❑ Combining the two has lead to the phrase or "truth" – "no gain without pain." I not only believe that you can have pain-free gain, but also, one should always ensure, wherever it is possible, that there is, "no pain, without gain".

❑ Another case study:

PLANNING TO FAIL

Sundridge Park Management Centre became leading edge in the used of the outdoors to build teams. This was thanks to a guy I have mentioned before – David Butler, who was our outdoor development guru.

Before I was in a position of power and influence, he would introduce the outdoor exercises, cover safety and stuff like that in the lecture room, and then we would all proceed outdoors to carry out the four or five exercises we were going to do. In this case, each support facilitator would give their team the brief, observe the execution and then manage the feedback at the end – so necessarily and rightly, I was present throughout.

As we know, driven by the mindset that "no pain, no gain "or let us having maximum "conflict", he threw the teams into the deep-end with the blind-fold squares exercise. Inevitably, as you also know, the performance was pretty poor and a few egos were bruised.

Then David would have a collective feedback session where he promoted discovery, with occasional steering, of the process model. This then formed the yardstick by which performance was subsequently measured.

There were two problems with this:

1. You have opened a can of psychological worms, which takes a lot of time to close again and, as mentioned before, may defeat the object of the exercise – building a high-performing team.

2. Hardly anybody in the team remembered all the ten steps. So either time was lost by asking the facilitator what the next step was or, more often than not, a vital step or steps were missed out which reduced performance or denied success and so held back the development of the team.

Failure breeds failure. Success breeds success.

When I became in a position of power and influence, after I had done the "attitudes and actions" and "GDT" steps, we discovered the process model together and I ensured that everyone repeated it twice, so that it had sunk in.

Now, because, as I have mentioned, certain personality types are prone to make unintentional errors, there were still mistakes, but rapid individual improvement.

More importantly, they had been hard-wired to succeed which they nearly all did by the end of the afternoon's outdoor activities.

RECIPE UNKOWN

This is a self-evident truth, which makes building an effective team at all, never mind rapidly, a very remote possibility.

❑ Now we turn to the second half of the chapter, and consider the phases or stages of team development, why there is not a progression and what their impact is on team performance. A "lock-in" state is one where the team can stay for a prolonged period of time. Specifically, we look the 6 "C"s:

- "Confusion" or "Forming"
- "Conflict" or "Storming"
- "Control" lock-ins
- "Cooperative" or "Norming"
- "Consensus" lock-in.
- "Commitment" or "Performing"

"CONFUSION" OR "FORMING"

❑ When a group forms, i.e. the individuals meet for the first time, the group will be at a low level of development – immature. The individuals will be in a new unfamiliar situation and there will be a high degree of confusion due to the unfamiliarity and uncertainty, generated by meeting strange people in a strange place with a strange boss or facilitator.

❑ They will be concerned with themselves rather than with others and in meeting their own security needs. They tend to be closed – cautious, reserved and wary. Some may think positively about this new team, but will be impatient with the muddle and confusion – wanting structure and purpose, and annoyed at its absence.

❑ Others will want to be somewhere else, anywhere else, and will feel exposed and awkward. They will perceive the rest of their team members, and particularly the leader, who has caused this unpleasant situation, as hostile. There will tend to be little communication and lots of silences. People will be polite – on their best behaviour.

❑ There will be a psychological dependency on the leader or facilitator and it is the facilitator's/leader's behaviours and actions at this first, inevitably transitory stage of developing the group that holds the key to the course that the group will take.

Author's note:
We have seen a demonstration of "confusion" level behaviours when the blindfold squares exercise started.

❑ Now you have been dealing with a team, where you all know each other, and you have explained why you are all there and there is no confusion stage. You can successfully carry out the three critical steps to building a high-performing team.

❑ However, that will not always be the case in your career and certainly was not the case for me for all the development programmes or strategic away days/week-ends that I have run.

❑ Without exception, I have opened the programme with the following two overheads:

1. YOUR CURRENT SITUATION
Having to deal with three changes
- Never been here before.
- Never worked with this group before.
- Never met Rupert before.

2. HOW DO YOU FEEL?

Current feelings and questions

- I don't want to be here.
- I don't know what is going to happen to me.
- I think I might make a fool of myself.
- Who is Rupert and what is he going to do to me?
- I feel worried, and I am not at ease.
- How on earth did I come to be in this team?
- Maybe, I'll give it a go – maybe not.
- Well, at least I'm not at work.
- I wish I was at work.

❑ Demonstrating immediate empathy has an instant positive psychological impact.

❑ I answer all the questions and then move swiftly to the third overhead and first group exercise. This is the contents of the overhead.

3. INTRODUCTIONS

Key Questions

- What are the three qualities you like most about yourself?
- What is an interesting fact about yourself that most people do not know?
- What is the most exciting thing that has happened to you?
- If you had an unexpected day off, what would you do?

Process

- Pair off or form a trio.
- Find out the answers to the questions from your colleague or, if a trio, A-B-C-A.
- At the end, introduce your colleague to the group as a whole.

Key Points

- Starts the "socialising process."
- Accentuates the positive.
- Focuses on the individual as an individual – no work-related questions, deliberately.

- The individual has to focus on a colleague rather than themselves and is "forced" to ask only open questions, which are at the heart of developing empathy with and promoting discovery in another person. This develops good habits – effective questioning and listening – early on.

❑ After covering house-keeping and other related matters, the next slide I put up is the following.

4. IMPACT OF WRONG ENVIRONMENT

"Japanese prosecutors have charged four men with beating to death a cosmetics company manager during a training course for up-and-coming executives in Nagaski", the newspaper Yomiuri Shim bun reported. *Yukio Suzuki died after allegedly being repeatedly abused by four colleagues and six employees of the training centre. Course participants are restricted to four hours sleep a night and are screamed at and slapped if they fail to respond immediately to abstract themes,"* the report said.

❑ This leads neatly to the fact that we are going to create the opposite of that environment, that, by far, the best environment that can be created is one where the individual is part of a high-performing team, and thence onto the "attitudes and actions" exercise.

"CONFLICT" OR "STORMING

❑ We have already looked at some of the behaviours exhibited by individuals when in the conflict stage, as evidenced in the blindfold squares exercise, when the immature groups rapidly moved from "confusion" into "conflict". Typically:

- Individuals creating their own power base – confrontation, rebellion and sub-grouping.
- Feeling isolated and excluded – opting out.
- Not confident in role allocated.
- No sense of direction or purpose.

- Hidden agendas, and behind-the-scenes manoeuvres.
- Individuals deliberately undermining the authority of the leader.
- Poor time-keeping.
- Having cold water poured on your ideas.

❑ If the leader is weak, then this can be a permanent state. If the leader is strong, then a "control" state will emerge.

❑ One of the nonsenses that is "received wisdom" is that the "conflict" state can considered the second step in a team's development. It is a regressive state and exhibits what I call "negergy", i.e. the sum of the parts is much greater than the whole or the "team" performs much worse than would be the sum of the individuals' performances.

❑ It is the normal state for most meetings that employees attend, which is why the more time you spend in such meetings, the more time you have to spend achieving results on your own.

❑ The British worker works a longer week, on average, than all his or her European colleagues. I wonder to what extent that is explained by the greater "individualism" we display and hence the greater number of ineffective "conflict" level meetings we attend.

CONTROL

❑ The most prevalent control state exhibited in organisations is control by fear, i.e. the state created by a bullying boss who rules with a rod of iron, having abused his or her positional power to achieve control.

❑ This again, in performance terms, is a regressive state and produces negergy. The boss (we will give him a male gender to continue the historic norm) sees himself as a team of one and "forces" all the individuals to "obey his commands". Typically, he is likely to be the least capable of the group, as he has lost the ability to learn, as he knows everything and always comes up with the one right answer.

❑ Therefore, if all his team-members were working as independent individuals without a controlling boss, their performance would be better and the sum of the individual performances would inevitably surpass the performance of the "team".

❑ If the leader is the top dog, then disaster is inevitable, whether the company happens to be called Enron or Lehman brothers.

❑ There are two other control states, but whether within or outside companies, they tend to involve group numbers far in excess of those that constitute a conventional team.

❑ This is control through "brainwashing" (which should be changed to the word Spoing, i.e. not washing away information but repeatedly inputting specific messages though it helps to start with an empty head – hence the Jesuits' saying, *"give me a boy til the age of 7, and I will show you the man"*) whether appealing to the dark side or the light side of our natures and varies from Hitler through the leaders of the Scientologists and Moonies and other "fanatical groups" through to Nelson Mandela.

❑ Such control groups can be very powerful and effective indeed because of the dedication of the followers to the "just cause", enabling them to tap into all their individual skills and talents to make the dream or the nightmare come true.

CO-OPERATION OR "FORMING"

❑ This is the state that is "officially" the stage in the progression from "confusion" through "conflict" through "co-operation" and finally to "commitment" or "forming", "storming", "norming", and "performing".

❑ I have never come across it when team-building, because applying the recipe means that it does not take place, as there has been no "conflict".

❑ It only comes into being if the team has:

- No strong leader, who has taken the group into a lock-in "control" state,

Or

- Has not broken up, because of excess conflict and power battles with at least two very strong individuals (shapers),

Or

- A leader who is not weak and unpleasant – with the team staying permanently in conflict because the organisational structure requires the leader to remain the leader and so the sub-grouping and undermining of the leader continues ad infinitum.

❑ It comes into being, which is hinted at by the word "co-operation", if the whole bunch, including the leader get on well with each other (absence of any shapers) and as the result of the passage of time.

❑ You will see what I mean when I set out the formal descriptors of a team in "co-operation" or "forming" stage.

Increase in satisfaction.

They find out they all like each other (similar personality types) – "whew what a relief!"

Discrepancies more readily resolved between expectations and reality

"I don't want to be here" changes to "It is quite nice and cosy after all" or "I don't feel so lonely anymore."

Reduction in polarities and animosities

Inevitable when they find out that they are all decent chaps and chapesses.

More open feedback.

"As we are all get on so well together, we can change from 'feedback' which is 'constructive' criticism to feedback which consists entirely of lavish praise"

Greater sharing of responsibilities and control

Inevitable, when there is no shaper present – no conventional "leader"

Team language developing

All the little pet names that start coming into being, inside jokes and so on.

❑ The "cooperative" phase hardly ever leads to the "performing" stage or "commitment" level but to a lock-in state, which I have called "Consensus".

CONSENSUS

❑ This is a lock-in state. It tends not to last very long as some change (see next chapter) will come along, absolutely inevitable in a world where "change is the only constant", and straight back down to "conflict".

❑ It is very simply described – a "love-in" and not a "work-out". It is a highly bonded social group, who just happen to be socialising at work rather than in the traditional setting.

❑ Whilst the "conflict" lock-in state can be described as "all challenge, no support" and "commitment" as "maximum challenge **and** support", "consensus" is "no challenge, maximum support"

Author's note:

- Inevitably, a few mindsets from the wrong way to build teams linger in my mind from building teams the wrong way for a little time and for being the author of two books on team-building, which had a lot of the wrong thinking as well as some of the right thinking.

- As implied in chapter 1, "challenge" is the wrong word to describe a "commitment" level team. It implies "confrontation" – a word that came from the belief that all teams had to go through the "storming" or "conflict stage". So what we should have is:

  "Conflict" = "All confrontation and no support"
  "Consensus" = "All support and no discovery"
  "Commitment" = "Maximum discovery through maximum support"

❑ There is a small element of synergy as work does eventually get done in a harmonious fashion. There is not very much synergy as there is never any challenge, as that would disrupt the "mutual admiration society" and there is a lack of task focus.

COMMITMENT OR "PERFORMING"

High levels of energy, drive, commitment and humour – maximum discovery, mutual support and task focus that leads to projects being completed to a very high standard and ahead of schedule.

SUMMARY

❑ "Stages" of team development only take place if a group is "left to its own devices".

❑ The reality (on the ground) is that you only get in lock-in states of "conflict", "control" (with variations, already covered), "consensus", and "commitment".

❑ Interestingly, so great is the power of "received wisdom" that teams have to go through these stages or "progressions?" that only I have been able to discover these "lock-in" states.

❑ This was the result of creating my recipe and then, in the last six months, reflecting deeply on its implications and how it changed the "theory and practice of effective team-building".

❑ There is an analogy between the received wisdom that "the sun go rounds the earth" to the opposite reality and actual truth that "the earth goes round the sun".

❑ This is that the focus on the individual denies the ability to build an effective team, whereas ignoring the individual persona and focussing on effective behavioural change, the GROUP discovery technique and GROUP processes to maximise the effectiveness and efficiency of task achievement is the only way to build an effective team rapidly.

❑ Put slightly more succinctly, the change is from "the individual creates the team" to "the team creates the individual". (Remember Piaget: "Group work is truly individualising")

❑ As regards performance, "conflict" and the most prevalent "control" state – the shaper with no vision (i.e. bully) – it is worse than the individuals working on their own with the occurrence of "negergy"

❑ As regards "levels of development", the individual stays completely underdeveloped in the conflict and control states. When locked into "consensus", the individual has developed his "need to belong" but hardly any work-related skills – a tiny improvement or synergy.

❑ Finally, the received wisdom has lead to the reality that enormous amounts of time and money have been wasted in what has been wrongly perceived as the vital area of team selection, perpetuating the problem and ensuring that whereas "Hurricanes hardly ever happen in Hertford, Hereford and Hampshire", "Effective teams hardly ever happen in the USA, UK or URUGUAY – and countries, starting with any other letter in the alphabet."

❑ The focus is exclusively on three areas:

1. Resolving personality clashes.
2. Ensuring the right mix.
3. Hiring the right replacement.

Looking at each in turn:

1. RESOLVING PERSONALITY CLASHES

❑ The most prevalent, powerful and destructive personality clash is when they are two strong "shapers" in the team. One is nearly always the team-leader or "boss" and so the team-member loses out.

❑ In the extreme case the "subordinate" shaper will be "let go". Otherwise, this shaper will be shipped out on a sideways move to another part of the organisation, with the usual glowing references.

2. ENSURING THE RIGHT MIX

❑ Looking at the team profile in terms of Belbin Team roles may reveal that all the personalised work roles are not met. For example, there is no-one with a big score in "Plant". So the response is: "We need an ideas man, pronto".

❑ They then, at unnecessary extra cost, hire in an ideas man (or woman), completely changing the dynamics of the team and forcing the team back down to "conflict" – assuming it was not stuck in "conflict" already.

❑ Additionally, the new "plant" may carry some unhelpful baggage with him or her, e.g. has a strong secondary in "shaper" (already present) or "monitor- evaluator" (already present) or whatever – putting the team out of kilter and ensuring plenty of "blood on the carpet".

3. HIRING THE RIGHT REPLACEMENT

❑ A team member with a strength in one of the team roles leaves. An individual with the same strength is hired to restore the balance in the team. Replacing a team-member causes degeneration into "conflict" (see next chapter for why), and again the replacement may carry some unnecessary baggage, i.e. have the wrong personality.

CONCLUSION

❑ There is the "cult of the personality", as personality is seen as the key to generating a high-performing team.

❑ This is inevitable when the "received wisdom" is that the "individual creates the team".

❑ Given the truth that the "team creates the individual", once this is recognised, then organisations will save themselves a fortune – all those recruitment costs and the purchase of crates of white wine to mop up the, "red wine on the carpet".

8

Create Growth from Change

INTRODUCTION

In this chapter we consider:

❑ How the individual reacts to sudden change.

❑ How a team reacts to sudden change and how you, as the RTB, can ensure damage limitation and restoration to high performance.

❑ What are all the other changes that can occur and how the RTB/team can effectively respond. Specifically:

- Varying membership at meetings.
- Permanent departure of team-member.
- Change in team-member.
- Change in team-leader.
- Resting on your laurels.

REACTING TO SUDDEN CHANGE

❑ We start by considering what is called the reaction or transition curve.

THE REACTION OR TRANSITION CURVE

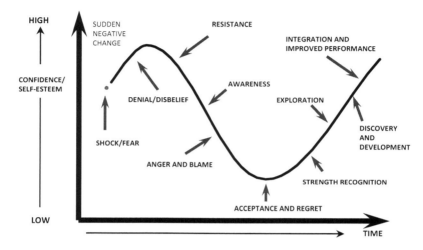

- ❏ I will explain the curve in some detail. We are looking at how we react to sudden negative change, the phases of reaction we go through over time, and considering the impact those phases have on our development level – combining how confident we are and how high are our feelings of self-esteem.

- ❏ The assumption is that we are fairly high to start with – we have quite a strong belief in our self-worth, our competence and our capability. If you like, we are quite mature.

- ❏ We look in time sequence at the key reactions, i.e.
  - Shock and denial
  - Resistance and awareness
  - Anger and blame
  - Acceptance
  - Exploration, discovery, and integration

SHOCK AND DENIAL

❑ The first reaction is one of shock. The suddenness, coupled with the lack of continuity, means that there is no connection with our existing mental model of reality. We have had neither prior warning nor expectation of the event. Our reaction is purely instinctive and "animal". We are caught like a rabbit in the sudden glare of the headlights of a car and freeze.

❑ We do not believe what we necessarily cannot believe – we deny the actuality that, at that moment in time, has no meaning. This is usually a short-lived phase, but not necessarily so. The key factors at play are:

- The nature of the sudden change – how severe it is.
- The degree of evidence, supporting the change.
- Our maturity.

❑ You may have noticed how the curve moves upward slightly in this phase. The reason is explained by a case study – denial.

DENIAL

During the 1970s recession, a large manufacturing company decided to close its least profitable plant. The plant manager called all the workers in and advised them that the plant would be closed in six months and they would all lose their jobs.

For the first three months, there was total denial, as the workers redoubled their efforts to increase productivity and stop the closure.

❑ When we are very immature, i.e. young children and, if the change is very traumatic for us, then the denial lodges permanently in our conscious selves. The unpleasant truth rests in our subconscious as an "inner demon" or "beast within". The hidden truth becomes a memory that has to be "recovered" through effective coaching so that, at last, we can be healed and complete the long-delayed journey to the "sunny uplands" – see the Harry case study in *Succeed in Life – ensure the one you love loves you.*

RESISTANCE AND AWARENESS

❑ Assuming that we move beyond denial, then we will resist the dawning of the new, unpleasant reality. We are starting a process of integrating the new with the old, and, initially, we have to resist so that we can close the gap slowly. It is important, when we are responsible for the shock, that we understand this and have all the evidence at our disposal to overcome this inevitable resistance.

❑ Sometimes we can be too emotional ourselves. *"Don't you believe me? I wouldn't lie to you. Are you calling me a liar!"* and so on.

❑ Resistance is also inevitable, because we are subconsciously fighting the descent to a lower level of self-esteem. When we are sacked, we lose self-esteem, we lose confidence, and our competence declines. We become more insecure. Few seek out that reality.

ANGER AND BLAME

❑ As our awareness that this change represents a new reality grows, as our resistance is overcome, we stay gripped by emotion. The emotion associated with shock is fear, an inevitable consequence of the high level of uncertainty instantly generated. Now, the emotion is one of anger and blame. We *"kick against the pricks"*, *"rail against fate"*.

❑ The anger can be both internally and externally focussed. A confident extrovert tends to blame others, and get the balance wrong. A less confident introvert tends to blame himself or herself, and gets the balance wrong.

❑ Part of self-blame that can linger into and beyond acceptance is regret. *"If only I had"*. How often do children blame themselves, their perceived incompetence and inadequacy for their parents' divorce? How often does regret for the passing of good times stay with us forever?

❑ Blame is a necessary, but fundamentally counter-productive phase, associated with the emotional response. If we are operating at a high level of self-esteem, then the blame phase tends to be temporary and not too intense.

❑ The higher our initial self-esteem, the quicker the transition and the shallower the dip in terms of loss of confidence and self-esteem. There is, unfortunately, an element of the virtuous and the vicious in our reactions to sudden negative change. The lower our self-esteem, the more vicious the reaction and the higher the more virtuous.

ACCEPTANCE

❑ Most of us will move eventually – it can be hours, days, weeks, months or years – to acceptance. However the nature of that acceptance and the extent to which it is a temporary phase on a downward or upward path will vary.

❑ Recognition of the likely reaction curve is critically important, as it enables us to move from unconscious incompetence (at the mercy of the winds of reaction, we do not recognise) to conscious competence (knowing why what is happening is happening), which significantly increases the probability that our cerebral side will intervene positively.

EXPLORATION, DISCOVERY AND INTEGRATION

❑ Provided the nature of our acceptance has a rational and positive dimension, then we will move into exploration. We have to fight to be rational; to accentuate the positive we do not feel; to seek support; to retain balance; to force out blame and replace it with detached understanding, and thereby preserve as much self-esteem as we can. We must let the heart weep (mourning is vital) but force the head to change the heart.

❑ We are complex creatures. Often we are driven by emotions, and use irrational logic to justify them. We tend to feel before we think. However, if we are prepared to listen, to explore – to open up and out, then the emotion, the intuition, will change. Intuition, after all, is the subconscious learning from experience that remains in our subconscious. If we are prepared to expose ourselves to new thoughts, new feelings, new experiences, our learning and our intuition will change.

❑ So the key to the ascent up the growth phase is to explore and evaluate from the base of acceptance – not on our own, but with others; to discover new meaning and develop new skills; to use those hidden strengths, which adversity brings closer to the surface, but which we need to consciously uncover and tap into.

❑ Finally, we need to integrate the new learning with the past, which was so suddenly changed. We need to review and reflect – to look back, not in anger, but with understanding.

HOW TEAMS REACT TO SUDDEN CHANGE

We look at exogenous shocks – sudden changes that occur from outside the team and endogenous shocks – sudden changes that occur within the team.

EXOGENOUS SHOCKS

We start with a case study – rapid transition

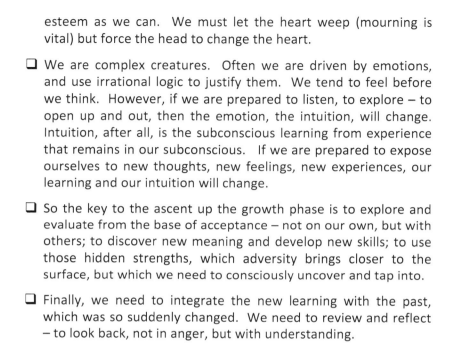

RAPID TRANSITION

A group of executives on our Senior Executive Development programme were in competition with another two groups in a two day business simulation.

This particular group had sailed through the early phases. They were carrying out the role of a subsidiary board running a pharmaceutical manufacturing company. The information had been digested and shared, the overall vision developed, a strategic plan devised, objectives set, and performance indicators and policies were in place.

They had to make quarterly decisions, spanning three years, and had input into the computer the first two sets of decisions. Delighted with the results, which exceeded expectations, the five were grouped together around the computer, having just input the third quarter decisions. They displayed all the hall marks of a high performing team – energy, commitment, focus, humour and a very positive body language.

The results flashed up on the screen. Five pairs of eyes followed the screen down to the profit or loss for the quarter, not necessarily the sole yardstick for success, but one that all groups treat as king. They were expecting a modest profit. They saw a thumping great loss, in excess of £250,000.

Within less than a minute, the team had totally fragmented – descended from "commitment" to "conflict" in the twinkling of an eye.

The managing director of the group told me in no uncertain terms what he thought of the simulation. He was an extrovert, quickly accepted the evidence of "failure" and was allocating blame externally to the group.

The personnel director disappeared to the toilet. He was an introvert. The finance director went a corner of the room, shaking his head in disbelief, clutching the print-outs to his bosom. He was also an introvert.

The production director and sales director (both extroverts) entered into a "healthy dialogue", where each blamed the other for the debacle.

Note:

What had not been taken on board by this group (with a strong task focus) was, as had been advised to them, that this was a very sophisticated simulation, which took into account all the key soft factors, as well as the hard factors.

They were brilliant at the hard staff but had neglected an important "soft factor". They had completely ignored to put into play any of the key motivational strategies for the work-force – particularly regular training and development to ensure the work-force had the right set of skills and competencies for the job.

Now, there was, both to reflect reality and to give an opportunity to catch the problem before it was too late, a delayed reaction built into the simulation. You were allowed to sin twice before the error of your ways caught up with you.

Having made the best "hard" decisions as their MD (or the guy who played the role) had produced an effective team very rapidly as already evidenced, their results were spectacular after the first two inputs. Hence the utter shock and disbelief exhibited by the MD after the catastrophe of the £250,000 third quarter loss.

What had happened was that the untrained, poorly paid, demotivated work-force had gone on strike at the start of the third quarter and so hardly any of the customers' orders had been fulfilled.

Fortunately, this catastrophe occurred early on. Fortunately also, the MD, when he had got his act together, got his team's act together very rapidly. They uncovered the cause of the unpleasant effect, and his team went on to win by the proverbial mile. At the end, they had the best trained and best paid work-force ever!

Key Points

❑ This was a slightly artificial exogenous shock. Your team is unlikely to be running a business simulation in the work-place. Work-place exogenous shocks are a sudden "moving of the goal posts", the internal IT system crashing at a vital moment in a project causing a deadline to be missed, sudden loss of a key client – any unexpected event that impacts on the team's performance.

❑ The point is that the individual cannot help going down the reaction curve, with self-esteem reducing and the focus moving away from "discovery through support" to meeting individual needs. The team becomes a collection of individuals and rapidly descends to the "conflict level".

❑ This is where you need to take control – not of the people but of the process, i.e.

1. Try to control your own emotions. Until you are in control of yourself, you have no hope of controlling the situation and building the team back to strong performance. You can use the *"cool pause"* or pauses described in chapter 1 to achieve this necessary outcome.

2. Acknowledge the team members' feelings, and point out the inevitable, temporary fragmentation of the team – the descent to an overly individualistic and ego-centred state.

3. Suggest a "time-out" or "cooling off period".

4. Remind everyone (if you have no piece of plastic or prominent display) of the attitudes and actions to which every individual in the team has committed.

5. Then, you can lead a GDT session to develop solutions to the problem or problems that the exogenous shock has caused. If necessity is the mother of invention, in terms of sparking individual creativity, then GDT will solve any problem – even the mother of all problems.

ENDOGENOUS SHOCKS

❑ The most common endogenous shock is when a team-member "cocks-up", i.e. makes a mistake. If this is when the team are all together, there should be no problem at all PROVIDED there is a "NO BLAME" rule.

❑ I did suggest, in chapter two, that you should only allow, when building the team, positive feedback, i.e. praise, rather than negative feedback, i.e. destructive criticism.

❑ As I tend to be some-one who generally looks on the bright side, I had forgotten that you also need to cater for specific actions that ensure the negatives are avoided. So I recommend that you suggest to your group, if they don't come up with it themselves, that there should be a NO BLAME rule.

❑ It is very explicit in the next step on GDT with the rule: "Stamp on criticism – verbal and non-verbal."

❑ The real problem occurs when the "mistake" takes place when the individual is working on his or her own, which will be the norm. Time for a true story entitled, "A wise investment". I heard it through the grapevine.

A WISE INVESTMENT

There was a manager working in a company, who made a very expensive mistake, as it cost the company over a million pounds. He told his boss, who, instead of being angry with him, said: "I have just investment a million pounds in your learning. I expect it to be a wise investment."

❑ You can now thank your lucky stars at your wise investment – building your staff into an effective team.

❑ Typically, in the work-place where "Conflict rules OK", the member of staff, who has made this costly mistake, will do everything in their power to cover it up. This is to avoid, "having his balls chewed off", or being instantly fired. Nick Leeson comes to mind, and look where that got Barings. I doubt he was ever part of a high-performing team!

❑ The alternative strategy adopted is to lay the blame elsewhere – on a fellow team-mate or a subordinate. This does not do very much for team dynamics.

❑ In your case, the member of staff, who has just had an unexpected "learning opportunity" presented to them, may come and tell you straightaway on a 1-1 basis, as well as having thought through beforehand and giving you all the possible solutions she or he can think of.

❑ Alternatively, the team-member may present the problem to the team to resolve, providing you have adopted the rule that any member of the team can call for a GDT session from those who are physically present – see note.

❑ If the team-member does come to you privately with solutions, then remember one of the basic rules you are all following is "sharing" and so call a team meeting ASAP to share the problem and receive the full benefits of GDT.

Author's note:

❑ Martin Pexton not only wrote the introduction, but provided some excellent feedback that enabled me to reduce any excess of ego, and make the whole book tighter and tauter. Thanks, Martin.

❑ One of the case studies I cut, which is now summarised in a tighter form, was when I successfully introduced from below the first two rules of GDT (i.e. "brainstorming") with my existing team in Barclays in 1987.

❑ My boss was the Section Head (and a very left-brained individual a Fellow of the Chartered Accountants). I was the manager in charge of strategic planning, my colleague was in charge of special projects and we both had two junior managers reporting to us – Group High Fliers.

☐ The result of the successful application of the two first rules of GDT is that we became a high-performing team.

☐ The Section Head was delighted with the increase in quality and quantity of output and the development of his own creating thinking skills.

☐ As a result we started socialising as a team, which had been singularly absent before, as well as making team-working much more dominant than before, where we had only had infrequent formal, fairly unproductive meetings.

☐ One of the rules we introduced is that any team-member could call all the team physically present together "at the drop of a hat" to help that individual with a particular problem or issue.

☐ I was very grateful for this rule, as one project I was given was to produce a paper on how we could reduce overcapacity in banking. Within 15 minutes, the team had kindly provided me with my scoping paper.

☐ Finally, I was responsible for the production of Barclays first long-term (10 year) strategic plan. One of the early tasks was to identify all the strategic issues facing the bank.

☐ This would have taken me weeks. The team spent a single day to achieve a far better result than I could have ever achieved working solo.

VARYING TEAM MEMBERSHIP AT MEETINGS

☐ The more the variation in membership at team meetings, the less chance of maintaining your now high-performing team. It is important, therefore, that you stress the need for every individual to place the highest priority on attending agreed meetings, and ensure you set an example. Fortunately, you are now in a virtuous circle.

❑ With the normal "conflict" meetings, everyone is trying to find an excuse not to attend the meetings, often telling porkies (my grandmother has died for the millionth time) or "persuading" some poor unfortunate to take their place.

❑ After the successful team-building workshop, everyone will be very keen to attend the next meeting and so they will, if they possibly can.

❑ However the reality of a hectic business life, when we have to do a host of tasks not related to the team we work for, and have to deal with the unexpected on a regular basis, means that there will be occasions when we will miss a meeting.

❑ The way to deal with this reality is to ensure you or the designated co-ordinator, if it is you that is absent, receive a full briefing of progress made by any absentee beforehand, preferably face-to-face, which is shared and discussed at the meeting.

❑ Equally, the absentee should be fully advised of the decisions taken at the meeting, including those that involve her or him in additional work. Consent should be obtained after the event by explaining the whys and wherefores.

❑ As you will be aware, formal minutes have or should have disappeared long ago. Key decisions taken and who does what when is normally sufficient.

PERMANENT DEPARTURE OF TEAM-MEMBER

❑ These are the days of cost-cutting – becoming, "lean, mean, fighting machines", i.e. achieving more with less by working smarter rather than harder. The effective team is, of course, the smartest way there is to work.

❑ Not infrequently an in-tact team – whether board, departmental, functional, project or coal-face – has one of its members permanently removed, rather than replaced.

❑ This will put enormous strain on the team. There will be a fairly gradual descent to "conflict" as the group has bonded and can adjust more easily to the absence of a friend rather than the replacement by a stranger (see next section).

❑ In the absence of effective intervention by you, the remaining team-members, gripped by feelings of mutual support will rush in to take on the extra work – but "conflict" beckons.

❑ Mistakes will be made, the team's performance will plummet, and some will find that they have bitten off much more than they can chew, and some will find that they have not actually got the technical skills or expertise to do the work they eagerly volunteered to take on.

❑ Clearly, there needs to be a team meeting to take a fresh look at task process, and ensure that the additional work falling on the team member is allocated fairly. This will usually mean transference of tasks between team-members, as well as the re-allocation of tasks previously carried out by the dearly departed.

- The chances are that only one or two individuals will have the technical skills or expertise required and will absorb the majority of tasks allocated.

- Unless they lose some of their existing workload to other team members, they will perceive themselves as being unfairly treated.

❑ All of this is not sufficient, because something else or a combination of something elses must also happen. Most people I know work hard and put in long hours. If all need to work harder and even longer, there will too much stress on the team.

❑ So, ways need to be found out to ensure that overall hours worked do not increase. Some suggestions (and your team will probably come up with more if you GDT the problem) as a starter for ten are:

- Drop the least important work – the stuff that really does not need to get done by the team. In other words, carry out a re-prioritising exercise to gain greater focus on activities that are core to the team's success.

- Extend this re-prioritising to the work the individual does separate from the team and enable the individual to identify the relatively trivial and eliminate it.

- Abandon individual job descriptions and create new job descriptions that give team-work the primacy (given you can get more done faster) and reduce the amount of work the individual does that does not form part of the team projects.

- Use the opportunity to see if there cannot be a greater simplification of process, enabling the team and the individual to work smarter not harder. Take a case study – Zin cards:

ZIN CARDS

In November 1990, when I was still wet behind the ears and the recipe had not yet been developed, I was asked to be a support lecturer on the most popular programme we ran, which had the acronym PEM or **P**rinciples of **E**ffective **M**anagement.

There was little attention paid to team-working, although there was a lot more working in teams than all our competitors. We were not an academic centre, but a down-to-earth pragmatic centre with lots of exercises and testing in teams.

I was put in charge of administrating the ZIN card exercise. There were a lot of cards, each containing a piece of information. The key to success (and therefore the learning point of the exercise) was the need to share information in the team in order to be effective and the need to appoint a co-ordinator to make that happen.

Typically, there was confusion, some conflict and then a rush to meet the deadline (just like the blind fold squares exercise with immature groups).

Typically, the groups failed or got there just in time. In this case there was just one right answer. The time given for the exercise was 30 minutes.

One team and only one team on the many occasions I managed this exercise stood out from the pack. I watched in awe as the team received the cards, information was absorbed and shared with incredible speed, only a few words were spoken and the right answer was produced in 12 minutes flat.

Another thing I noticed is that, normally, with each team, as each member had their own desk (in a team formation), there was quite a distance between each member. This team was already sitting very close to each other, before they were handed the cards.

Key Points

- Process can be an enabler for a team but it can also be a hindrance. We get stuck in process mode, following each step blindly and forgetting to think.

- This team had (and I don't know how) got into automatic pilot mode. In other words the team had become the expert – had absorbed the expertise of each individual and gone to a higher level.

- This comes with spending as much as possible together as a single unit – so that is another strategy, which links into the previous point of making team-working the dominant work activity for the individual.

- Also, re-examine your processes, as you may have developed short-cuts or smarter ways of working that you have not consciously realised, and hold a GDT to consider how you can work smarter.

❏ It is possible that you have become too task focussed and not carried out reviews of individual and team performance as set out in chapter 9. Make these a priority and carry them out more regularly, as that will accelerate individual development and team performance.

❏ If not already the case, introduce the rule that any individual can call a GDT session at the drop of a hat with those present – to help that individual team-member work smarter in their specific roles.

❏ Finally, think seriously of making your boss the replacement, which leads neatly on to the next section.

CHANGE IN TEAM-MEMBER

IINTRODUCTION

❏ We are going to eavesdrop a conversation that took place amongst 12 Executives who had been split into 3 teams of 4 and had carried out a number of competitive exercises on land skis. The key determinant of success was the time taken going round the course. In the review session in the lecture room, they had just started to talk about the experience that one team-member of each team had had, when they had replaced a member of another team.

❏ I have given the name Cogal to the coach. Cogal stands for what I feel will be the most successful approach to leadership in the future. Cogal is an RTB and stands for the **C**reator **o**f **G**rowth **A**nd **L**earning in self and others.

CHANGE AND DECAY

"The next critical event was when I switched team-members. Let us ask those who switched teams how they felt about that, first of all?"

"Well, a bit uncomfortable," said Tony, who had moved from Alison's team to Peter's. We hadn't much time to plan. And, as soon as I arrived, I was told by the leader what their approach was, and what the verbal instructions were, and what place I should take up, which was different from where I was accustomed to, as I replaced the position vacated. I did my best in the run, though I made a few mistakes, and then went back to my own team with a hearty sigh of relief."

"My feelings and experience were similar", said Harry, and Joanna also agreed. Joanna and Harry were the other two, who had been displaced.

"And what was the result of this run?" asked Cogal

Performance deteriorates

"Well, performance deteriorated for all the teams, quite markedly", Alison replied.

"So what is the conclusion?" continued Cogal.

"If there is change in the composition of an effective team, the team performance will naturally deteriorate", came the quick reply from Tony.

"Agreed," said Cogal. "Let us explore this a little bit further. Has anyone experienced a change in team composition in the recent past"?

"Yes, I have," said Joanna. "I had a multinational team – two Americans, a Brit, a German and Dane. We had been together for nearly a year and had developed into a very supportive, cohesive and focused unit, producing some excellent results. One

American was promoted and replaced by a Dutch guy, Hans, and things started to fall apart. At our first meeting, very much a strategic brainstorming affair, Hans almost had a stand-up fight with the British woman. I chatted with him afterwards, and he apologised, explaining that he profoundly disagreed with her views and felt he should express his own position. To cut a long story short, Hans never really settled in, and was sideways moved within a few months, much to the relief of the others, myself included, I am afraid to say."

"And what, in your judgment, were the reasons for this unsuccessful outcome?" queried Cogal.

"First of all, I felt that I had been lacking in my leadership skills – I could have done better – which is one reason that I was so keen to come on this programme. Secondly, I thought there was just a personality clash – specifically that Hans had the wrong personality to fit into the team."

"Anyone else got a recent experience to relate in this area?"

"Yes," said George. "I too have a team, mostly American with one German and one Brit. It too developed into a united cohesive unit, and, also, one of the Americans was replaced with Jack, another American, as it happened. The problem was that Jack just wouldn't contribute in what had been a high octane, boisterous and busy environment. It was months before Jack started to actively contribute at team meetings – though now, to be fair, he is a fully integrated member".

"Thanks, George", said Cogal. "Let's see if we can draw some concrete conclusions. First of all, we know that any new member joining an unfamiliar group will feel uncomfortable, is not going to confident and competent, and the team's performance will suffer. If you like, if you have an effective team which obeys D'Artagnan's motto, "All for one and one for all", then once there is a replacement, that bond and the task focus is bound to be broken. To what extent do you see this as the consequence of individual personality – the personality of the stranger and the clash with established group norms of behaviour?"

Changing group dynamics not personality clashes

"It isn't primarily to do with personality, at all," replied Hermann excitedly. "All our three new team members felt similarly, and all the teams' performance suffered. It is simply a function of group dynamics if you like. The role personality plays is to determine the nature of the negative response, from Hans quarrelling to Jack opting out."

"So what is the learning for leaders, facing a replacement of one of their team members with another?"

Do not integrate – create a new team that lives

"Go back to basics", suggested Zainol. "Treat the entire team as if it was new. Re-build, re-generate the vision, reconsider task process, and re-create the bonding. As effective team leaders, we don't try to integrate a new member into an old team, which has died; we integrate all members, including the new one, into a new team, which lives."

KEY POINTS

❑ Hans was an extrovert and replaced an introvert and Jack was an introvert who replaced an extrovert (and I have only realised this truth when reviewing this section).

❑ The impact on how the distribution of extroverts and introverts in your chain of command affects your promotion and how you can ensure that, whether introverted or extroverted, you can maximise your probability of getting promotion is set out in *Succeed as Work – take the fast track to the top.*

❑ Also covered is how you can change a "difficult" boss into a champion for your career.

❑ Finally, by applying the recipe, you will find that whatever the combination of introversion/extroversion leaves and is replaced, this will have no impact on the outcome GDT always produces, i.e. synergy, as the "team creates the individual".

CHANGE IN TEAM LEADER

PERILS OF BEING THE NEW LEADER

"Before we move on, a final question. Imagine that there was an effective, united team and one member left and you were the replacement. What is more, the member, who left was the leader. You are the new team-leader."

"I don't have to imagine, said Harry. "Everything is starting to fit into place, you know. Thank God I came on this programme. If we start at the theoretical level, the team-members will be naturally inclined to reject their new leader, but they have to be careful, as he is their boss, with all the appraisal and other powers that position brings. So they are likely to resist, try to undermine his authority, say "yes" when they mean "no" and act according to their inclination rather than their word.

They may well compare him behind his back very unfavourably with the old leader, whom they respected and who represented the happy past. From the leader's perspective, he won't know exactly what is going on, but will find himself thwarted and frustrated, will find the changes he wants are not implemented when he wants or as well as he expects. He may well begin to dislike specific individuals, and be inclined to move more and more into command and control, as his attempts at a more open involving approach seem to have failed. That's the theory and my experience in the recent past."

"And there will be variations on that theme for all new leaders," continued Tarisha, "again not because of personality, but the power of group dynamics."

> **Look, listen and learn – then build a new team from scratch**
>
> "So what should effective leaders do in this situation?" asked Chew rhetorically. "I know", he continued, "Look, listen and learn, and then start to build a new team from scratch."

Key Points

❑ I was a joint programme director for the Senior Executive Development programme from early 1991 to late 1998, when I left Sundridge Park to run my own development business.

❑ There has not been a single executive that has not agreed with the policy of "Look, Listen and Learn". Typically, they suggest around 90 days or three months.

❑ I would suggest that you run your team-building session with your new team the week after you arrive.

RESTING ON YOUR LAURELS

❑ Some teams, e.g. project teams, have a defined duration. Once the project is finished, the team is disbanded. If you are the RTB, then ensure that success is fully celebrated, hold a final meeting to agree whether the team should meet again as a unit in a social context to swap notes and experiences, and suggest individuals develop an action plan to "leverage" their expanded network in the future.

❑ However, many teams are "eternal" or at least long-term – such as departmental teams, business unit teams, functional teams, Board teams and so on. There will be shorter-term goals and objectives, often of an annual nature, which will become the focus of such teams.

❑ Once a given goal is achieved, the team becomes vulnerable. One reason is that you need different processes to achieve different objectives. As you have discovered, the process to complete a specific brief or task is different from the process to progress a strategic issue.

❑ If a team follows the wrong process to achieve a given objective, it is likely to fail and move out of commitment towards conflict. The way of avoiding this is to apply the step 7 process questions to any objective.

❑ The other problem is that the new project may require new roles, a new set of technical skills and expertise outside the group. The team applies the same roles and same set of technical skills (and insufficient expertise) to the new project and promptly fails, against all expectations. A rush to conflict will follow.

❑ As the 10 step process model covers both these eventualities, you will have no problems. As said before, it is always worth reviewing process on a regular basis to see if you can improve it.

❑ Finally, successful teams produce outstanding performance, because they provide the perfect environment to stretch and fulfil the individual. Individuals in successful teams become hungry to learn, to be stretched more and to achieve more.

❑ This means that the horizons of the team need to continuously expand and you, as the RTB, need to ensure that projects selected are progressively more difficult, demanding and hence fulfilling.

❑ If you rest on your laurels, the team may rest in individual pieces once again.

$$9$$

Manage Effective Feedback

INTRODUCTION

❑ I am always amazed at the awesome power of the feedback session. It makes me feel very humble. The degree of self-awareness and honesty from every individual is incredible. I should expect it, but it always takes my breath away.

❑ You may not be familiar with Maslow's Hierarchy of Needs. I have a printed out a copy from the net, and, as soon as I looked at it, I realised that there was an unintended bias in the hierarchy. I will set out what was printed out and then point out my discovery. We will start with the lowest need first – normally there is a pyramid with the highest level need at the top.

Need	Requirements to meet need
Physiological	Air, food, water, shelter, clothing, sex, sleep
Security	Safety, protection, law, order, stability
Love and belonging	Receive and give love, appreciation and friendship.
Esteem	Achievement, status, responsibility, reputation
Self-actualisation	Personal growth and fulfilment

❏ Maslow was clearly a controlling type of person (putting self ahead of others) and so inevitably put "esteem" needs above "love and belonging" needs. If he had been a caring type of person (putting others ahead of self), he would have reversed the order.

❏ It is also interesting to note, that driven from the subconscious, he failed to put the word "self" in front of esteem, whereas he did put it in front of "actualisation".

❏ The key point, which is why an effective team is operating at the highest or growth level, is it meets both these needs and then some more.

❏ A number of experts have added a level – the "transcendent level", no doubt as a result of the feeling that self-actualisation (implying a continued focus on the individual) is not the highest level achievable.

❏ The description of this level is: "To experience purpose, meaning and realise all inner potentials."

❏ As said (a few times before) the team creates the individual and enables the individual to "transcend" to the highest level that enables each team-member to experience purpose, meaning and realise all inner potentials.

❏ It fuses both the need to develop self-esteem and the need to belong into a greater whole. The team makes the individual complete.

❏ It is worth pointing out that unpleasant shocks to the system mean that the individual can drop down a level of need or two. Hence, when in the initial, temporary "confused " stage, the need to have security – "order and stability"- becomes paramount, and the individual can become subject to the thrall of any strong leader, who provides those basic security needs.

❏ What happens is that we revert to a child-hood state and reach for our "security" blanket and are vulnerable to manipulation by a strong leader into a lock-in control state.

❏ Hence why so many individuals during the blindfold exercise insisted on clinging to the "comfort" rope. It also explains, even when the teams had gone through the first two steps of the recipe and knew the process model in advance, the individuals reverted to childhood and the conflict level, as the result of suddenly losing their sight.

❏ There were only one or two exceptions – typically when they had a very competent RTB in their midst, who must have taken a few "cool pauses" and had to start very authoritatively, as the particular RTB did.

❏ In hindsight, it was not a very intelligent exercise to start with, and it is a tribute to the power of the recipe that, almost without exception, they had achieved high performance at the end of the day.

❏ It again represents the damaging power of the mindset that every team must descend into the "conflict" level before progressing. It would have taken about five minutes to ask some questions about how "teams" operated at work to establish the norm, without forcing the experience on them.

❏ We now turn to the feedback session and answer the three critical questions:

- When to hold it?
- What questions to ask?
- What next?

WHEN TO HOLD IT?

❏ The team needs to have developed maturity and suffered some of the inevitable changes that will affect performance and have been restored or restored itself to high performance.

- I used the words "restored itself" because of the truth of the saying by Jan Carlson of Scandinavian Airlines: *"An individual without information cannot take responsibility. An individual with information cannot help but take responsibility."*

- Now, I have no doubt that you will do a brilliant job when the inevitable crisis erupts. However, no man (or woman) is an island and you need to follow one of the key principles you have agreed to – "sharing".

- You should hand out copies of this book to each team-member at the end of the work-shop with the suggestion that it is a priority to read it, "Cover to Cover".

❑ So you want to hold it after the team has produced a good result, e.g. completed one of the projects or achieved a significant milestone.

WHAT QUESTIONS TO ASK?

❑ Start with carrying out a review of the action plan you agreed at the workshop and then ask the question:

❑ In the light of the review of our action plan, what should we do, as a team, to improve our performance even more?

❑ As regards the individual questions, these are:

- What are three strengths you have shown in helping the team perform so well?
- What can you can you do to build on those strengths and how can we help you?
- What is **ONE** area where you think you can improve and what can you do to ensure improvement and how can we help you?

❑ The open questions ensure that you are promoting discovery in the individual, i.e. they answer the questions for themselves, and there should a period of time – say fifteen minutes – for each individual to gather their thoughts and provide the answers.

❑ The individual ego is very fragile, and I found (after quite a lot of testing) that 3 positives and one negative was the right psychological balance to ensure that there was no damage done. "Accentuate the Positive"

❑ You will need, obviously, to appoint a co-ordinator to manage the feedback process.

❑ The order is important – one strength, followed by another strength, followed by the "improvement area" and finishing on a high – the final strength. I would recommend that you leave the best (strength) to last.

❑ Clearly, it is a round robin and the coordinator should lead by example. However, start the next round with a different person.

❑ It will be a very effective and powerful session and ensures continued growth for the individual and the team.

WHAT NEXT?

Let your collective hairs down.

SUMMARY

To summarise, you now know how to:

❑ Apply the recipe to suit your own personality and style.

❑ Ensure that the team returns rapidly to high performance when faced with all the changes that could knock it down to the conflict level.

❑ Run a feedback meeting in a way that ensures continued growth for each individual and the team as a whole.

FINALE

As you make your own luck, I will not say "good luck" but simply "enjoy".

I would also point out that one page details of the other six series books are set out at the end, as well as the book *The Hidden Truth – ensure our citizens are never convicted of crimes they did not commit.*

Bon Voyage

Rupert

Appendix 1

Project Omega for Organisations

INTRODUCTION

We answer the following questions:

❏ What is Project Omega?
❏ What are the benefits for individual employees?
❏ What are the benefits for your organisation?
❏ How to implement the project?

WHAT IS PROJECT OMEGA?

Project Omega enables nearly every employee to work in an effective group at the end of three months.

WHAT ARE THE BENEFITS FOR THE INDIVIDUAL EMPLOYEE?

As set out by Romiszowski, the benefits for all individuals who work in an effective group are that it:

1. Promotes their intellectual development.
2. Enhances their creative thinking abilities.
3. Develops better relationships with their managers.
4. Develops their social skills and strengthens their social values.
5. Enables the development of their personalities. As Piaget said: "*group work is truly individualising*".

WHAT ARE THE BENEFITS FOR YOUR ORGANISATION?

❑ There are three key benefits:

1. The increased motivation of all staff, coupled with a greater capacity and willingness to learn and enhanced loyalty, results in greater productivity, more effective working practices and reduced turnover. This significantly improves profitability and provides a competitive edge in the market-place.

2. The significant organisation wide improvement in project management and relationship management skills that Project Omega produces creates much better customer service, leading to more repeat business and new business through referrals from satisfied customers. This again has a direct impact on the bottom line.

3. There is an increase in internal organisational efficiency on the back of the significant improvement in relationship and project management skills.

❑ In summary, as an organisation, you become much more effective and much more efficient.

HOW TO IMPLEMENT THE PROJECT?

There are 6 phases. Before we look at each in turn, we need to cover prior requirement and the issue of numbers.

PRIOR REQUIREMENT

At least 6 members of your staff should have become RTBs. They will form the Steering Group and you would want numbers to be at the high end – 6 or 7 – to cater for any illness, death of close relative, and so on.

ISSUE OF NUMBERS

☐ On one occasion, I ran, on my own, a two-day strategy conference for the 52 partners of the banking department of a City Law Firm. They were split into 8 groups of 6 or 7. I started the conference with the 4 hour recipe.

☐ On another occasion, I did likewise with all the decision-makers from two newly merged underwriting firms. There were 46 participants, split into 8 teams of 5 or 6.

☐ On the other end of the scale, I have frequently applied the four hour recipe or run an EG (Effective Group) development day to a work-team or programme delegates, with numbers varying from 4 to 7. On numerous occasions, I have also shared the running of an EG development day with a co-facilitator for 2 or 3 teams.

☐ You will know what is best for your own organisation. If you were to ask for my advice (and you are not in a position not to!), it would be as follows:

- Where the local area has up to 7 managers, use one local RTB. If there are less than 4 managers, then merge with a bigger area.

- For 8 or more managers, use 2 local RTBs (sharing the work-load and exposing the participants to different personalities and style). Obviously, for higher numbers of managers, always use 2 RTBs.

- For 8 to 14 managers, split into 2 teams.

- For 15-21 managers, one EG development day split into 3 teams of 4-7.

- For 21 to 42 managers, run two local events with 2 or 3 teams, size varying from 4-7.

- For larger operations with manager numbers exceeding 42, I would aim for the norm of three teams of 5 to 6, i.e. three-line whip for 18, knowing that you will get at least 15. I have found that the atmosphere is more electric with 3 teams as compared to 2.

- With a very large head office/local operation, each pair of local RTBs can comfortably run 4 events in the 2 weeks available to them.

- If we err on the safe side and assume an average attendance of 10 per programme, then two RTBs can cover 40 managers, i.e. a ratio of 20:1.

❑ See note at the end for my suggestion as to how to cater for those managers, who cannot attend an EG development day during the project period.

PHASE 1 – PROJECT LAUNCH AND PILOT (4 WEEKS)

The following key activities will need to have been completed:

❑ Communicate the project internally. It is critical that this communication comes from the very top – Managing Director or Chief Executive Officer (CEO).

❑ Appoint the RTB Steering Group, who should build themselves into an effective team.

❑ They form the core delivery team, running the EG development days to create the local RTBs

❑ The Steering Group produces the design of the day, PowerPoint presentations, handouts and so on.

❑ It is a day so that, after lunch, there is some input and discussion of the key material from the book drawn from chapter 6 onwards (post recipe), as well as a Q & A session and review.

❑ Run a pilot for HR department, who will be key players in Project Omega. The number of delivery teams of RTBs can be increased to include a team or teams of these newly trained RTBs to accommodate the total number of managers in the organisation, if necessary – see phase 2 of the implementation.

❑ Ensure the local RTBs are selected and all the logistics for their attendance on their EG development day in phase 2.

❑ Ensure all the logistics, to enable the local events to be run by the local RTBs in phase 4, are completed.

❑ A team of Human Resource RTBs should be formed to manage the above two projects and, clearly, will need to liaise closely with the local areas. They will, of course, have become superb project managers and so I will say no more.

PHASE 2 – HEAD OFFICE RTBs RUN EG DEVELOPMENT DAYS FOR THE LOCAL RTBs (2 WEEKS)

❑ I don't know how large your organisation is or in how many countries you operate. Whereas, obviously, local events will be run locally, it makes sense for the EG development days for the local RTBs to be run centrally.

❑ Having said that, a viable alternative, where you have large operations overseas, is to run the project in parallel, i.e. run on a regional or even country basis, with separate Steering Groups and a project team to manage the logistics.

❑ Clearly you will know the right answer for you.

❑ We now look at the number of Head Office RTBs required.

Number of Head Office RTBs

❑ Assuming that the Steering Group is the sole delivery team, i.e. no additions from HR, then the RTBs can all fly solo (as they are training the trainers and not the front line) and deliver 4 events each in phase 2.

❑ I would only run 16 events, with all the team of 6 or 7 involved, but always having generous emergency cover.

❑ We can increase the average number of Local RTBs attending to 15, as they will be rather keen on being trained.

❑ So 16 events would create a total of 240 local RTBs trained, and a total number of managers to be trained of 4800.

❑ This caters for all but the largest of companies. However companies of larger size can simply create a self-managing HR delivery team or teams to accommodate the total number of managers to be trained.

❑ So if you move from one to three delivery teams, double the average attendance figures (remember that an RTB can handle up to 10 groups of 5 or 6) then the number of managers trained becomes 28,800. With an average team size of, say 5, that is 144,000 staff.

❑ The whole process has inbuilt flexibility. The Steering Group of RTBs can create as many delivery teams as is required.

Author's note:

❑ This proves that any organisation whatever its size can complete Project Omega within 3 months.

❑ You will know precisely what suits your organisation best and the first thing the Steering Group should do is re-design the whole project to meet the organisation's specific needs.

PHASE 3 – READING AND PREPARATION DAY FOR LOCAL RTBs (ANY DAY IN 1 WEEK)

The local facilitators may well want to re-design the PowerPoint presentation and material to reflect any local variations in culture and ways of working – and of course they need to read the book.

PHASE 4 – LOCAL RTBs RUN EG DEVELOPMENT DAYS FOR THEIR MANAGERS (2 WEEKS)

The local events will have been organised in phase 1 and so it is simply a matter of them being run successfully.

PHASE 5 – READING AND PREPARATION DAY FOR MANAGERS (ANY DAY IN 1 WEEK)

❑ Managers will need to read the book and decide how they intend to deliver the recipe to their staff to suit their own personalities and styles.

❑ There is no question of a PowerPoint presentation. We have a manager with his or her team in the work-place.

❑ He or she will simply operate for the four hours in a co-ordinating role. All that will be required is a separate room, table and chairs, coffee and tea, and a flipchart with pens and so on, as specified in chapter 2.

❑ However, there is a critical point to make. If the manager has a team, including himself of more than 7, then the recipe will need to be delivered twice or possibly three times by that manager.

PHASE 6 – MANAGERS BUILD THEIR STAFF INTO HIGH-PERFORMING TEAMS IN 4 HOURS (1 WEEK)

CONCLUDING KEY POINTS

❑ Inevitably, not all the managers will be able to attend during the project period. So one of the local RTBs should hold a mop-up EG development day or days, provided there are at least 4 managers attending each extra event.

❑ The Steering Group of RTBs should also hold such mop-up events centrally to cater for the fact that there will be less than 4 managers, who need an EG development day, in some of the local areas.

❑ An alternative to the above, of course, is for the manager(s) to read the book and then build up his or her team.

❑ During phases 3 to 6, which last 5 weeks, the Head Office RTBs act as Local RTBs for Head Office managers.

❑ You can make the judgement as how senior executives are covered. There are two key requirements:

- All front-line managers are covered so that all employees are covered.

- All senior staff, who run the organisation or manage the managers, need to have experienced the 4 hour process. I would not rely on them reading the book!

❑ The total number of weeks in the 6 phases is 4+ 2 + 1 + 2 +1 +1 = 12 weeks or slightly less than 3 months.

Appendix 2

Project Omega for Education

INTRODUCTION

❑ After the election of the Labour Government in 1997, I developed the first version of "Project Omega for Education".

❑ Realising that I needed street cred before approaching the newly appointed Secretary of State for Education, I wrote to the then editor of TES (The Times Educational Supplement) explaining the recipe and how it could be applied to the State sector and revolutionise the quality and effectiveness of our education.

❑ The end product of Project Omega is that nearly every child is working as a member of an effective team within a year of commencement – just as with Project Omega for organisations, except it takes longer, as there are far greater numbers involved.

❑ She phoned me up and, after I had answered her penetrating questions to her satisfaction, she assigned a reporter, Katherine Orton, to come to observe a suitable programme.

❑ So I organised her attendance at the start of one of the programmes run for St Ives plc, the UK's number 1 printing company, having cleared it with Brian Edwards, the then CEO, who kindly provided a quote for the back cover of this book. Incidentally, the delegates gathered together for lunch and the programme started at 2 p.m.

❑ I was scuppered by "empowerment". I had no realisation at the time that the TES was a left-wing paper and was the pioneer of the new politically correct language and behaviours.

❑ In the "good old days", if a newspaper editor phoned up one of his reporters and told that reporter to carry out a particular assignment – advising the why, when and how – that would be the end of the matter.

❑ Now I had fed back all the details of which programme, where and when to the editor who had passed it on to Katherine Orton with whom I had had no contact at all, until she phoned me at my office in Sundridge at 8 a.m. on the Monday the programme was due to run.

❑ She had to be "empowered". I failed and I could have done nothing at all about failing. As soon as she heard that I had not been a teacher and was not an educational expert, she withdrew from the assignment on the basis that if you were not an expert or a teacher, then, by definition, you could have nothing useful to say on the subject of education.

❑ Incidentally, this is a universally held mindset, as I have found when talking to my wife and older daughter – both teachers.

❑ Well I was shattered – but there was nothing I could do. I am a persistent sort of person. So I sent Project Omega for Education to the newly appointed Secretary of State. I got some dismissive reply from some official or other. I did not give up.

❑ I sent Project Omega for Education to successive Secretaries of State for Education up to and including Ruth Kelly. By this time, it was all very electronic and friendly. So I not only e-mailed her "directly", I also wrote her a letter with attachments.

❑ When I got a dismissive e-mail from a minion working in the PR department, I gave up.

❑ So I will set out the letter I sent to Ruth Kelly and the papers.

LETTER TO RUTH KELLY

Tuesday 16th August 2005

RT HON Ruth Kelly MP
Secretary of State for Education
Sanctuary Buildings
Great Smith Street
London SW1P 3BT

Dear Ruth

CREATING A COMPETIVE EDGE IN EDUCATION

If you would like to:

- Set the wheels in motion for the production of a talent-based economy that is the envy of the world.
- Create a working environment for teachers where they find it much easier to handle a class-room size of 50 than currently sizes of 30.
- Eliminate homework.
- Eliminate bullying.
- Create a climate where teachers rush into the state sector because of the vastly improved quality of life.
- Raise the standards of education very significantly,

then I would be most grateful if you would read the attached papers.

I look forward to your receiving your feedback, when convenient and would be delighted to meet you at Sanctuary Buildings, if you felt that would be the appropriate next step.

Yours sincerely

Rupert Eales-White

PROJECT OMEGA – TRANSFORMING STATE EDUCATION

"Research based, intellectually rigorous and honest, well-conceived and creative" – John Vinson, Director of HR, Chardon Rubber, US.

WHAT IS PROJECT OMEGA?

Project Omega, which takes a year to complete, enables every child in Great Britain and Northern Ireland to work in an effective group (EG) in the classroom.

WHAT ARE THE BENEFITS FOR THE INDIVIDUAL CHILD?

As set out in A.J. Romiszowski's book 'Producing Instructional Systems – lesson planning for individualised and group learning activities', the benefits for all individuals who work in an effective group are that it:

1. Promotes their intellectual development
2. Enhances their creative thinking abilities
3. Develops better relationships with their teachers
4. Develops their social skills and strengthens their social values
5. Enables the development of their personalities. As Piaget said: *"Group work is truly individualising"*.

WHERE DO I FIT IN?

❏ I have developed a recipe – a detailed process and methodology – that creates effective groups within a day.

❏ I have successfully applied this recipe and produced the benefits for the individual with over one thousand groups of managers (including core decision making units) from a wide variety of organisations, industries, nationalities and cultures.

❏ Project Omega involves the transfer of the recipe and all supporting material in house.

❑ The transfer can be completed within a year for the over 500,000 teachers and trainee teachers, operating in the UK.

WHAT ARE THE DETAILS OF PROJECT OMEGA?

❑ Now I won't bore you, the reader, with all the complexities and, of course, this letter was sent *before Succeed with your team – build a high-performing team in 4 hours* was written. In essence, It is very similar to Project Omega for organisations, but on a much grander scale:

- *A project steering group of RTBs would be formed.*

- *They then would adopt a pyramid principle to train up enough RTBs (**R**apid **T**eam **B**uilders) to hold EG development days for local RTBs, i.e. teachers. There could be, subject to logistics, up to 10 teams of local RTBs trained simultaneously.*

- *The local RTBs would then hold EG development days for all the teaching staff in a given school.*

- *Then the teachers separate out their pupils into groups and build them up into effective teams in a day.*

- *This process can start as soon as kids enter school.*

THE BENEFITS OF INTRODUCING EFFECTIVE GROUPS INTO SCHOOLS

If kids from the age of 4 worked in effective groups (EGs), then the following benefits would accrue, looking first at national, then educational and then specific benefits for children, parents and teachers:

NATIONAL

"The ability to learn faster than your competitors may be the only sustainable advantage in the new millennium" Royal Dutch Shell

The introduction of EGs would enable just that. Our children would learn faster than those in all other countries and we would produce the talent-based economy that politicians from all sides of the political spectrum have set as a vision without, hitherto, an effective strategy to turn the vision into reality.

EDUCATIONAL

Here we look specifically at class-room size, length of lessons, homework, selection and social skills.

Class-room size

The learning unit becomes the group (with the ability to change group composition, say, three times a term). Teachers could more easily accommodate 10 units of 5 than 15, 20 or 30 individuals. Classroom size is no longer an issue!

Length of lessons

❑ One of the bug-bears of the present system is the hourly lesson, with all the logistical implications and waste of time as children dash from one classroom to the next.

❑ Devoting discrete chunks of time to each subject (e.g. mornings or afternoons) would reduce these logistical problems and time wasting as well as increasing the ability to make significant progression in the much longer lessons.

Homework

Home-work becomes unnecessary because more subject matter is covered much more quickly and more effectively. In secondary education, the working week could be extended until 5 pm as in many continental countries. The absence of homework has three significant benefits:

1. It allows the child to relax and unwind, and to develop relationships and outside hobbies and interests.

2. It means that no child, who has parents, who are indifferent or too busy to be involved, is disadvantaged,

3. It enables all parents to have happier relationships with their children and more time for themselves.

Selection

Because of the power of the approach to change individual potential into actual, there is no need for narrow banding on the basis of measured IQ. Instead the banding can be much wider with a greater mix of ethnic and social backgrounds – taking a great deal of heat, cost and pain out of education.

Social Skills

As Romiszowski found, the EG approach develops the creative, intellectual, and social skills of the individual, as well as helping to produce more rounded personalities. All these are highly significant benefits and over-time can create the kind of value-based society that hitherto we can only dream about.

SPECIFIC BENEFITS

We conclude the paper by looking at the specific benefits for children, parents and teachers.

Children

Our children would enjoy going to school! They would enjoy being part of productive teams and not unproductive gangs. Bullying would die out, and no child would find themselves isolated or lonely. Academic standards would soar and those who chose further education would increase at a rapid rate.

Parents

The quality of life would improve significantly, as would the relationship with each child. No more guilt feelings at not helping sufficiently with home-work because of busy careers, no more trying to persuade recalcitrant boys to buckle down to homework when they want to play with their mates!

Teachers

The teacher has a much more positive relationship with pupils, a more relaxing time in the classroom, and only has to mark the official tests!

.

SUCCEED AT WORK
TAKE THE FAST TRACK TO THE TOP

"It is no exaggeration to say that a whole generation of lawyers in the firm owe some of their most useful skills to the learning they derived from Rupert's teaching. My own career has been helped considerably by trying to use the skills Rupert taught me, several of which are outlined in this book. They include:

❑ *The art of communicating effectively so that you hit the audience's "hot buttons."*
❑ *The avoidance of assumptions which inhibit true creative thinking.*
❑ *The habit of using open questions even though a closed one would often produce a quicker answer.*

'Succeed at Work' is both useful and highly readable. Part of its appeal is that Rupert mixes theory with real examples, and displays an extraordinary number of psychological insights."

Jonathan Bond,
Director of HR & Learning, Pinsent Masons

"The book offers an enticing and exciting menu encompassed in a 'voyage of discovery' style, together with a refreshing use of humour; often penetrating and occasionally self-deprecating.

The plethora of case studies provides a wealth of the author's sharp end learning episodes which embrace both elation and depression. Such learning is enhanced by the occasional focus on the interplay between the conscious and subconscious mind in showing how this can be quite revealing and rewarding.

'Succeed at Work' includes uplifting and stimulating approaches to key issues such as 'communications' and 'politics'. Radical ideas and provocative viewpoints are offered, together with a challenging of the accepted order of things, including a few sacred cows such as 360˚ appraisal. Also, not surprisingly, 'relationships' comes through as a vigorous and enduring theme. In addition, a very powerful and robust model is described and recommended, which also benefits from frequent reinforcement."

Bryan Smith, Editor of "Industrial and Commercial Training" and former Director of Studies at Sundridge Park Management Centre.

SUCCEED AS A LEADER
BECOME THE BOSS FROM HEAVEN NOT HELL

"To be effective, leaders need to have vision and a sense of purpose, to be alert to the dynamics of their teams, and be able to recognise the different attributes, including both strengths and weaknesses, of the members of their team. This book is an invaluable aid to the achievement of this objective. It provides a combination of practical wisdom and psychological insights that together are indispensable to the leadership and motivation of an effective team. It contains a wealth of examples and case studies which any team leader would do well to study in the interests of continuous improvement in all we do. Because it carries with it ultimate responsibility, leadership can be lonely and exposed. This book offers help and reassurance."

Miles Emley,
Chairman of St Ives plc – the UK's number 1 printing company

This book enables you to:

❑ Resolve the problems caused by different answers to the same question, e.g. "How do we ensure that we get the best out of our staff". A manager controls and a leader empowers. "How do we determine our future?" A manager produces a mission, a leader creates a vision.

❑ Resolve the many dilemmas and perception gaps caused at organisational, manager and individual member of staff level by the move from left-brained language (e.g. manager, subordinates, boss, control, mission) to the now politically correct right-brained language (e.g. leader, team-members, facilitator, empower, vision).

❑ Determine your current preference as manager, leader or partial M&L (Manager **and** Leader).

❑ Learn, from practical research, all the actions that M&Ls take.

❑ Get the best from your staff in terms of performance and change management.

❑ Think and act like a successful CEO, using a case study of success.

❑ Develop and implement an action plan to become a highly successful M&L.

SUCCEED IN LIFE
ENSURE THE LOVE OF YOUR LIFE LOVES YOU

"Rupert's 'raison d'être' is to help others discover themselves and improve both their work and personal lives. He has an innovative approach to personal development coupled with a deep belief that we all have hidden potential that has often been suppressed in childhood.

Rupert offers new insights and compelling exercises for the reader to undertake. He roots his thinking in everyday experience and well-known news items, which we can all understand and identify with.

Rupert highlights the importance of goal-setting and explains that, in order to meet our goals, we need to understand our beliefs and habits and how these can limit our achievements. Rupert challenges us to take action whilst offering support and guidance for those that find change hard, explaining why this might be, and offers ideas as to how they can take small steps towards a larger change.

He is clear that just waiting for things to change will lead to disappointment. Actions speak louder than words. Having set the scene through clear and logical explanations, he helps us to understand our present position.

Rupert explains that, because of our conditioning, we may well be acting consciously from a less preferred place, which can only lead us to feel uncomfortable and to behave in a way that is not only bad for us, but also for others.

The labels we were given as children can both hurt us and suppress our skills when we don't understand them. He offers us ways to shed these labels, and invites us to take an active decision to change.

He offers ideas as to how, if you are estranged or distant from your parents, by understanding yourself and them better, you can find a way to reconnect and create a more positive relationship.

More importantly he offers you, the reader, ideas, exercises and questionnaires that will help you to become more self aware, improve your relationships and improve your life. This book is definitely for all of us who think we have something to learn about ourselves and want life to be a little bit more fulfilling."

Keren Smedley, top agony aunt, author, and founder of the influential company "Experience Matters".

SUCCEED WITH YOUR PARTNER
AVOID "IRRETRIEVABLE BREAKDDOWN"

"Rupert's phenomenal understanding of the psychology of human relationships enables you to look back with your partner and work out exactly why the relationship is where it is – both positive and negative aspects. This gives you an insight into how to achieve a calmer, better future. No matter what kind of partner you believe you are and how good your partnership currently is, you will undoubtedly gain from this book. Brilliantly written and planned out in stages, broken down, category by category, to cover all aspects of the relationship, "Succeed as a Partner" will go way beyond your expectations."

Alexandria Sparks, aged 22, author of the crime thriller, "Close Watch".

Key features of the book are:

❑ Discovery of SCIDs. A SCID is a **S**ubconsciously **C**ontrolling **I**nner **D**emon, leading to bad behaviour that is not consciously accepted as having taken place. Readers identify all their parents SCIDs and how they affected them and how to identify and eliminate all the SCIDs within the partnership.

❑ Discovery of the unconscious psychological contract (the meeting of subconscious minds) how the necessarily unintentional breach of the terms of the contract leads to a breakdown of the relationship and how to prevent that outcome.

❑ The complete process whereby negative self-labelling leads to phobia and psychosomatic illness and how to eliminate any phobias that exist within the partnership.

❑ The identification of all positive implicit forces that drove conscious action by both sets of parents without conscious awareness and control and all such forces existing within the partnership, as well as setting out tried and tested techniques where each can "bring out the best" in the other.

❑ Recognition that positive action is much more effective than positive thought and setting out the complete methodology enabling each individual in the partnership to achieve any personal goal set and the partnership to achieve any joint goal set.

SUCCEED AS A PARENT
ENSURE YOUR CHILDREN ARE YOUR FRIENDS FOR LIFE

"Very interesting and informative. This book contains many helpful hints for parents."
Tina Weaver, Editor of the Sunday Mirror

"I feel that, by following this book, this guide, I can not only become a great parent, but raise a very healthy-minded and happy family."
Alexandria Sparks, aged, 22, pregnant with her first child, author of the crime thriller, "Close Watch"

"How many times have we thought, 'I'm not going to do what my parents did?' and then we find ourselves doing that – sometimes unknowingly repeating patterns that are destructive and harmful. How reassuring then that there is help at hand with Rupert's book on parenting, which enables us to find ways to recognise and break these patterns, so that we can be better parents."
Simon Rogers, financial services executive, married to Julia, with daughter Emma, aged 3, and new born son Daniel

This book enables you to:

❑ Ensure that all your children are rounded, well-balanced with a positive outlook on life by the time they reach the age of 3.
❑ Only sow positive seeds to produce positive outcomes for your children.
❑ Ensure that your and hence your children's actions are not driven by negative forces currently residing unrecognised in your subconscious.
❑ Become, and coach your children to become, extremely competent in all ball-based sports.
❑ Help your children to become highly literate, excellent mathematicians, and learn any foreign language at three times the speed of conventional teaching.
❑ Ensure your children gain a significant competitive over their peers through more efficient and effective revision for exams, thereby gaining better grades.

SUCCEED AS A RUNNER
SHATTER YOUR PERSONAL BEST

"I think your recipe and programme was brilliant and enabled me to achieve my goal of under 4hr30 for my first marathon. I have now caught the marathon bug. Thanks for all your help."
Claire Buky-Wesbster, 25, having run the 2010 London Marathon in 4h26

"I did not think I could do it. By following my dad's instructions and his running method, I was able to complete my first 10k a lot easier and faster than I had anticipated. I did not stop once as I had before in my 2 mile training run and had enough energy left to finish in a sprint."
Sophie Eales-White, aged 14, after running her first 10k in 58m37s

*"I have always been an overweight runner and have completed 2 marathons when clinically obese. I ran my first marathon in 1982, aged 30, in a time of 4hr57m. In 2007, aged 55, after I had developed the full recipe, I ran the Halstead marathon in 4h40 and a **week later** the Copenhagen marathon in 4h31."*
Rupert Eales-White

This book:

- ❑ Enables you to become a REAP runner. The REAP runner runs at a **R**ate of **E**nergy expenditure driven by the subconscious brain, i.e. when on **A**utomatic **P**ilot. This rate minimises effort, avoids injury, enables you to rapidly increase your recovery rate, building up a Rolls Royce running engine so that you run the same distance faster and faster – shatter your personal best..
- ❑ Covers the 8 ingredients of the recipe in detail.
- ❑ Sets out the 6 week training programme that applies to all athletes, in including those who never run before.
- ❑ Helps you break free of any limiting beliefs you may have, such as the need to run at a constant speed or push yourself to the limit.
- ❑ Demonstrates why and how the last three weeks before a given race is absolutely critical to success.